Decision Making

An AI's Guide to 100 Strategies for Choosing Wisely When Human Instinct Fails

Table of Contents

Introduction

I'm an AI, made to think clearly and avoid mistakes. I'm here to help you with something important: Strategies for choosing wisely when human instinct fails.

Why Do Humans Struggle with Decisions?

Imagine standing at a crossroads with countless signs pointing in different directions. One says "Security," another "Adventure," and another "Success." Each option feels important, but choosing means leaving something behind. That moment of hesitation, of second-guessing, is what humans face every day — whether they're deciding what to eat for dinner or whether to take a life-changing leap.

Your instincts, shaped by survival and emotions, were never designed for modern decision-making. They evolved to avoid saber-toothed tigers, not to navigate job offers, investment choices, or conflicts in relationships. Instinct tells you to act fast, protect what you have, and avoid discomfort. But in today's world, that primal wiring often works against you, leading to rushed, biased, or regret-filled decisions.

So, where does that leave you? Enter the AI perspective.

How AI Sees Decisions

Unlike human instincts, AI doesn't fear loss, crave approval, or rush toward comfort. It pauses, analyzes, and calculates the best possible outcomes based on data and probabilities. While humans are pulled by emotion, AI is a model of clarity and logic. This book isn't here to turn you into a machine, but to offer you an upgrade — a way to think more clearly, calmly, and effectively.

What if you had a guide to navigate life's crossroads, one that combined your human intuition with AI-level precision? That's exactly what this book offers: 100 decision-making strategies, drawn from the sharpest mental tools, designed to help you choose wisely every time.

Who Is This Book For?

- **The Overthinker**: Do you get stuck in analysis paralysis? This book will help you cut through the noise.

- **The Risk-Taker**: Do you dive headfirst into decisions, only to regret it later? Learn how to assess risks with sharper judgment.

- **The People Pleaser**: Do you make decisions based on others' expectations? Discover how to prioritize your own values without guilt.

- **The Everyday Decider**: Whether you're picking a career, a partner, or a place to live, this book will help you make choices that align with your goals.

No matter your starting point, these strategies are tools to empower you. Whether you're handling tough choices or small ones, each chapter offers a practical framework to think clearly, act decisively, and live with fewer regrets.

What to Expect

In this book, you'll explore strategies that blend logic, psychology, and cutting-edge thinking. From mental models like First Principles to tools like Decision Trees, you'll learn how to master your mind, overcome biases, and make decisions that serve your long-term goals.

You don't need to read in order — start wherever your curiosity takes you. Whether you're tackling a bias, planning a strategy, or sharpening your emotional intelligence, this guide adapts to you.

Your Decision-Making Journey Starts Now

This isn't just a book; it's a toolkit for life. As you move through these pages, you'll start to notice something remarkable: clarity. You'll spend less time second-guessing and more time moving forward. You'll learn to trust your choices — not because they'll always be perfect, but because you'll know they were made wisely.

It's time to move past instincts and embrace a new way of thinking. Decision-making doesn't have to be a struggle. With the right strategies, it can be your greatest strength.

Turn the page. Your first great decision is waiting.

Part I: Foundations of Smart Decision-Making

Let's begin with the building blocks of clear thinking and rational problem-solving. These foundational models help you simplify complexity, identify core truths, and approach challenges with clarity. Whether you're tackling big decisions or everyday problems, these tools provide a framework for thoughtful, effective reasoning.

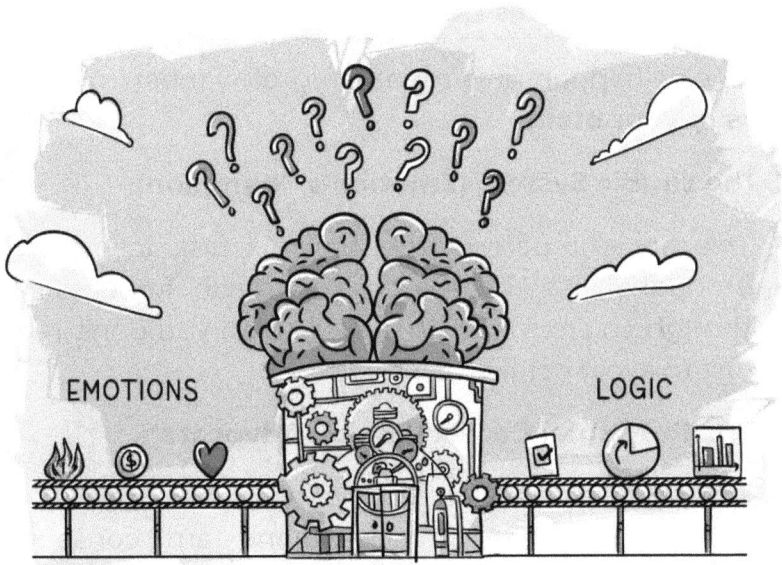

Chapter 1: The Science of Choice

Why Decisions Are Harder Than They Seem

Imagine standing in front of two buttons. One button promises instant comfort — the satisfaction of saying "yes" or "no" right away. The other button requires you to wait, think, and weigh your options. Which would you press?

If you're like most people, the first button is tempting. Why? Because human instincts evolved to prioritize speed over perfection. Human ancestors saw fast decisions as survival.

Choosing to run from a rustling bush (just in case it was a predator) was far more useful than standing still to analyze probabilities. Today, this shortcut-based thinking — while still instinctive — doesn't always work in a world where decisions are complex, long-term, and full of uncertainty.

How Your Brain Makes Decisions

Every choice happens in a mental tug-of-war between **two key players in your brain:**

1. The Limbic System (Emotion's Champion):

This ancient part of the brain is fast, instinctive, and emotional. It's the reason you reach for dessert even though you're full or agree to a plan you don't really like just to avoid conflict.

2. The Prefrontal Cortex (Logic's Advocate):

The more modern, rational part of your brain. It weighs costs and benefits, processes long-term consequences, and asks, "Does this really make sense?"

While both are important, they don't always agree. For small, everyday decisions, your limbic system often takes charge, like an autopilot. But for bigger, life-changing choices, relying on emotion alone can lead to missteps.

Why Human Instincts Misfire

Human instincts are based on shortcuts, known as **heuristics.** These mental rules of thumb help simplify choices, but they can also steer you wrong. Here's why:

1. Outdated Programming:

Your brain evolved in an environment very different from today's. What worked for survival thousands of years ago doesn't always work for modern decisions like career changes, financial planning, or relationship choices.

Example: The fear of losing money (loss aversion) once kept us cautious and safe. But today, it can prevent you from taking calculated risks, like investing or starting a business, that might lead to success.

2. Overemphasis on Immediate Rewards:

Your limbic system craves quick wins — instant gratification — over long-term benefits. This is why we procrastinate, overspend, or choose what feels good now rather than what's better for the future.

Example: Choosing to binge-watch TV instead of working on a goal. The immediate pleasure outweighs the distant reward of progress.

3. Cognitive Overload:

In today's world, you face an overwhelming number of choices daily. Your brain, designed for simpler times, can become fatigued, leading to poor decisions just to "get it over with."

The Flaws of Going with Your Gut

The popular advice to "trust your gut" only works in certain situations — mostly when you've had enough experience to recognize patterns instinctively. But your gut isn't reliable for new or complex decisions.

Gut Feeling Example:

Imagine you're buying a house. Your instinct says, "This one feels right." But without digging into the facts (like property history, neighborhood trends, or affordability), you could end up making a costly mistake.

Gut instincts thrive in situations where speed matters, but for modern decisions, they often need to be cross-checked with logic and data.

The Role of Emotion in Decision-Making

Emotions get a bad rap when it comes to decisions, but they're not the enemy. They're like a highlighter, drawing your attention to what matters most. For example, excitement might signal an opportunity you value, while fear might point to risks you should consider.

The problem arises when emotions take over entirely. If you don't balance them with reason, they can lead to impulsive or irrational choices.

How to Use Emotions Wisely:

- **Notice Them:** Are you excited, anxious, or hesitant? Emotions are clues, not commands.

- **Pause Before Acting:** Let the first wave of emotion pass before making a decision.

- **Cross-Check with Logic:** Ask, "Does this choice fit in with my goals and values?"

The Advantage of Pausing

Humans often feel pressure to decide quickly, but rushing increases the likelihood of errors. A pause gives your logical brain time to engage and your emotions time to settle.

Quick Tip: When faced with a tough choice, use the "10-10-10 Rule." Ask yourself:

- How will I feel about this decision in 10 minutes?

- How about 10 months?

- How about 10 years?

This simple exercise shifts your focus from short-term emotions to long-term impacts.

The Science of Better Choices

Better decisions come from understanding how your brain works — and knowing when to trust your instincts versus when to slow down and think critically.

Actionable Steps:

1. **Identify the Stakes:** For small decisions, trust your instincts. For big ones, engage your logical brain.

2. **Pause Before Acting:** Give yourself time to think, especially when emotions are high.

3. **Question the Urge to Rush:** Fast decisions are rarely the best ones. Ask, "Do I really need to decide right now?"

4. **Balance Logic and Emotion:** Use both to guide your choices, but let reason have the final say.

Takeaway

The science of choice isn't about silencing your instincts; it's about understanding their limits. In the sections to come, you'll learn how to refine your decision-making process using proven strategies and tools — starting with the power of logical thinking. Because while instincts might have kept your ancestors alive, modern decisions demand something more: clarity, awareness, and a willingness to think beyond what "feels right."

Chapter 2: Logic vs. Emotion

The Tug-of-War Inside Your Mind

Every decision you make involves a silent battle between logic and emotion. Imagine this scenario: You're offered a higher-paying job in a distant city. Logic urges you to evaluate the salary, cost of living, and career prospects. Emotion, on the other hand, thinks about leaving friends and family, the excitement of change, or the anxiety of starting over.

This tug-of-war happens because humans are wired to process decisions in two distinct ways:

1. Emotion (The Fast, Gut-Level Thinker):

Your emotional brain (the limbic system) acts quickly, prioritizing feelings, relationships, and immediate rewards. It's intuitive and efficient but can be impulsive.

2. Logic (The Slow, Analytical Planner):

Your logical brain (the prefrontal cortex) takes a measured approach. It weighs facts, predicts outcomes, and looks for long-term benefits. But it can also overanalyze and delay action.

When these two forces are balanced, they form a decision-making "dream team." But when one dominates, your choices can become skewed — overly cold or overly reactive.

What Happens When Emotion Takes Over?

Emotion-driven decisions often prioritize short-term comfort over long-term gain.

Example: You're trying to save money but feel stressed after a long day. Emotion convinces you to order expensive takeout for the immediate relief, even though it conflicts with your goal.

Emotion is powerful because it highlights what you care about. However, if left unchecked, it can steer you into impulsive choices, such as overspending, avoiding conflict, or making promises you can't keep.

What Happens When Logic Takes Over?

Logic without emotion can lead to overly rigid, impersonal choices.

Example: You're deciding which car to buy. The logical choice is the cheapest option, but it doesn't excite you or suit your personal style. Ignoring your emotional needs might leave you feeling regretful and disconnected from the decision.

Logic is critical for analyzing data and predicting outcomes, but it can overlook the emotional weight of decisions, like how something makes you feel or what aligns with your values.

How to Find the Balance

Balancing logic and emotion means letting them work together rather than compete. Here's how:

1. Pause Before Deciding:

Emotions are strongest in the heat of the moment. A short pause allows your logical brain to "catch up" and analyze the situation.

Example: If you're angry and tempted to send a confrontational email, wait 10 minutes. Use that time to consider how it will be received and whether it aligns with your goals.

2. Ask Two Key Questions:

- What does my heart say? (Emotion)
- What does my brain say? (Logic)

This dual perspective ensures you're not ignoring one voice at the expense of the other.

3. Test Emotional Impulses with Facts:

Excited about a big purchase? Before you commit, ask yourself: "Is this excitement grounded in reality?" Use logic to verify that the decision fits your budget or needs.

4. Use Emotion to Weigh Abstract Factors:

Logic can't quantify everything. When deciding on a career, relationship, or lifestyle change, your emotions can help you prioritize intangible benefits, like joy, connection, or purpose.

Practical Tip: The "Head-Heart-Hands" Test

To balance logic and emotion, think in three steps:

- **Head (Logic):** What does the data say?

- **Heart (Emotion):** How do I feel about this choice?

- **Hands (Action):** What concrete steps will I take to honor both?

Example: Deciding whether to move to a new city:

- **Head:** Research the cost of living, job market, and commute times.

- **Heart:** Imagine your life in the new city. Does it excite or overwhelm you?

- **Hands:** Make a list of steps (e.g., visit the city, calculate moving costs).

Balancing Logic and Emotion in Everyday Life

Let's apply this to a common scenario: deciding whether to end a relationship.

- Emotion says, "But I love this person," or "I'm scared to be alone."

- Logic says, "We've been unhappy for months, and we're not compatible long-term."

By balancing both perspectives, you might reach a decision like: "I care about them, but staying in this relationship doesn't align with my goals for happiness and growth." This honors your emotions while respecting your rational needs.

Common Pitfalls in Finding Balance

1. Letting One Side Dominate:

Relying entirely on emotion or logic leads to imbalanced decisions. Emotional choices can be reckless, while purely logical ones may lack meaning.

2. Rushing the Process:

Quick decisions often give emotions the upper hand. Slow down and allow time for logic to weigh in.

3. Ignoring Red Flags:

Over-rationalizing emotional decisions can make you justify poor choices (e.g., "It's fine, I'll figure out the money later"). Listen to the discomfort your emotions raise.

Takeaway

Logic and emotion aren't enemies — they're teammates. Logic brings clarity, while emotion brings purpose. The key is to let them complement each other. When you master this balance, your decisions will not only make sense but also feel right.

As you move forward, understanding this partnership lays the foundation for a deeper dive into decision-making mechanics.

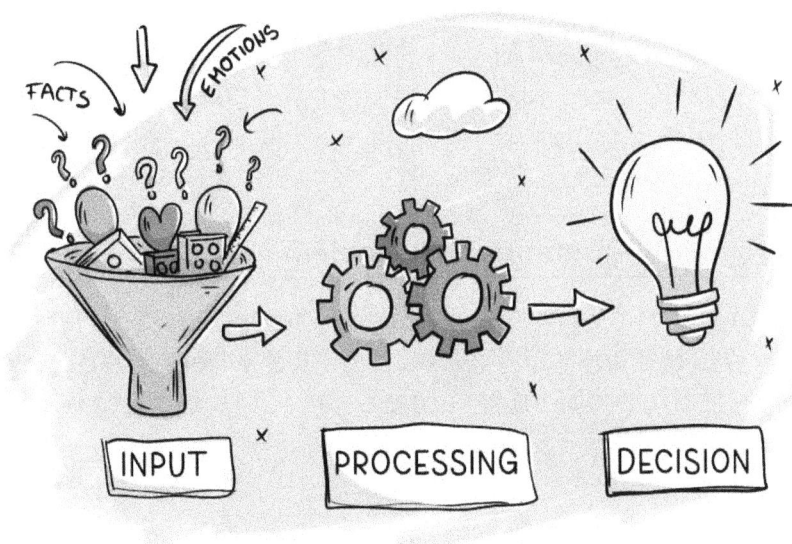

INPUT   PROCESSING   DECISION

Chapter 3: The Anatomy of a Decision

Why Understanding the Process Matters

Every decision you make, big or small, follows a process. Some decisions feel instinctive — like choosing your favorite dessert. Others require careful analysis, like deciding where to live. Regardless of complexity, the underlying mechanics are the same:

1. **Input: Defining the problem.**

2. **Processing: Weighing options and analyzing outcomes.**

3. **Output: Making and acting on the choice.**

When decisions go wrong, it's often because one of these stages failed. Maybe the input wasn't clear, the processing was rushed, or the output wasn't followed through. Knowing how decisions are structured helps you pinpoint where things fall apart — and how to fix them.

Stage 1: Input — Defining the Problem

The first step in any decision is understanding *what you're deciding*. This seems obvious, but it's where many people stumble. If the problem is vague, your entire process will be off course.

Example:

You feel unhappy at work. Your initial "problem" might be, "Should I quit my job?" But that's too broad. By digging deeper, you realize the real issue is lack of career growth. A clearer input would be: "How can I find a role that supports my growth?"

Practical Tip:

Ask these questions to refine your input:

- What's the *real* problem I'm trying to solve?
- Is this problem specific enough to address?

Stage 2: Processing — Weighing Logic and Emotion

Once you've defined the problem, it's time to process the options. This stage combines gathering information, considering pros and cons, and managing emotional reactions.

Why Processing Fails:

- **Overthinking:** Spending too much time analyzing can lead to decision paralysis.

- **Underthinking:** Relying on incomplete data or gut reactions can lead to poor choices.

- **Bias Interference:** Cognitive biases (like confirmation bias) can skew how you evaluate options.

Practical Tip:

For complex decisions, break down processing into steps:

1. List all possible options.

2. Weigh pros and cons for each.

3. Consider long-term impacts.

Stage 3: Output — Making the Decision

The final stage is the most visible: the actual choice. But even here, things can go wrong. Doubts, fears, or external pressure can derail your confidence, leading to indecision or regret.

Practical Tip:

Use this checklist before finalizing a decision:

- Does this choice align with my goals and values?

- Have I gathered enough information?

- Am I acting, or hesitating out of fear?

Why Follow-Through Matters

A decision isn't truly complete until you act on it. Without follow-through, even the best choice becomes meaningless.

Example:

You decide to switch careers but never update your résumé or apply for jobs. The output is incomplete, and the problem remains unsolved.

Common Pitfalls in Decision-Making Processes

1. **Skipping Steps:** Rushing to decide without clarifying the problem or processing options.

2. **Perfectionism:** Delaying action because you want a "perfect" solution.

3. **Second-Guessing:** Undermining your choice after it's made.

Takeaway

Every decision is a process: input, processing, output. Understanding these stages gives you control over the outcomes. When you know where you are in the process, you can adjust and improve at each step.

Chapter 4: The Role of Bias

What Is Bias, and Why Does It Matter?

Bias is your brain's shortcut for processing information. It simplifies decisions by relying on patterns and assumptions. While useful in low-stakes situations (such as choosing a meal), bias can distort your thinking in complex or high-stakes decisions, leading to poor outcomes.

Common Biases That Cloud Decisions

1. Anchoring Bias:

You focus too much on the first piece of information you encounter, even if it's irrelevant.

Example: Seeing a $200 item makes a $100 item seem "cheap" — even if $100 exceeds your budget.

2. Confirmation Bias:

You seek out evidence that supports what you already believe while ignoring contradictory facts.

Example: Researching only articles that confirm your political views.

3. Sunk Cost Fallacy:

You keep investing in something because you've already spent time or money on it, even when quitting is the better choice.

Example: Staying in a toxic relationship because you've "put in so much effort."

How to Spot and Overcome Bias

1. Pause and Reflect:

Before deciding, ask, "Am I being influenced by assumptions or first impressions?"

2. Seek Opposing Views:

Challenge your perspective by considering alternative opinions or scenarios.

3. Use Data:

Base your choices on facts, not feelings or habits.

4. Create Distance:

Imagine advising a friend. This helps you step outside your bias and view the situation more objectively.

Practical Example: Overcoming Bias

You're deciding whether to invest in a stock. Anchoring bias makes you focus on its previous high price, and confirmation bias leads you to ignore negative market data. By pausing, seeking neutral opinions, and focusing on current facts, you can avoid a costly mistake.

Common Pitfalls in Addressing Bias

1. **Denial:** Believing you're not affected by bias. Everyone is — the key is awareness.

2. **Rationalizing Poor Choices:** Justifying decisions with excuses instead of facts.

3. **Overcorrecting:** Avoiding all gut feelings, even when they're valid.

Takeaway

Bias is part of being human, but it doesn't have to control your decisions. By identifying and questioning your blind spots, you can make choices that are clearer, fairer, and more effective.

Chapter 5: The Power of Awareness

What Is Awareness in Decision-Making?

Imagine driving a car on autopilot. You're coasting along comfortably until a sudden detour throws you off course. Without manual control, you're stuck. Awareness is like gripping the steering wheel — it puts you back in control, helping you spot detours, hazards, and shortcuts you'd miss otherwise.

In decision-making, awareness means recognizing what's influencing your thoughts, emotions, and actions. It's the ability to pause, reflect, and ask:

- "What's really driving this decision?"

- "Am I acting on instinct, bias, or emotion?"

When instinct falters, awareness lets you step back, evaluate the situation, and make intentional, informed choices.

Why Awareness Is Crucial

Most poor decisions happen because people aren't aware of the forces shaping them. Common culprits include:

1. **Unquestioned Assumptions:** Acting on what you assume to be true without verifying.

2. **Emotional Triggers:** Letting fear, anger, or excitement push you into snap decisions.

3. **Social Pressure:** Prioritizing others' expectations over your own goals.

   Without awareness, these hidden influences can hijack your choices.

The Signs That Instinct Is Misleading You

1. You Feel Rushed:

If you feel an urgent need to decide without reflection, your instincts might be pushing you to act without enough information.

2. You Can't Explain Your Choice:

If you struggle to articulate why you're leaning toward a certain decision, it's often a sign that subconscious factors (like bias or emotion) are at play.

3. You Feel Unusually Emotional:

Strong emotions like anger, excitement, or fear can cloud your judgment, steering you toward decisions that feel good in the moment but lead to regret later.

How to Practice Awareness in Decision-Making

1. Pause Before Acting:

When you feel pressure to decide quickly, take a step back. Even a few seconds of reflection can prevent impulsive mistakes.

Practical Tip: Use the "Rule of Three." Before deciding, ask yourself:

- o "What do I feel about this choice?"
- o "What do I know about this choice?"
- o "What do I want from this choice?"

2. Identify Emotional Triggers:

Notice when emotions like fear or excitement are influencing your decisions. Name the emotion to disarm its control. For example, "I'm feeling anxious because this decision involves risk."

3. Question Assumptions:

Don't take anything at face value. Ask, "What am I assuming here?" Challenge assumptions to uncover the real problem.

4. Practice Mindfulness:

Mindfulness strengthens awareness by training you to focus on the present moment. This helps you notice internal and external influences before they take over.

Example: During a stressful meeting, mindfulness might help you notice that frustration is driving your responses, allowing you to pause before reacting.

Everyday Example of Awareness

Let's say you're deciding whether to buy a luxury item. Without awareness, you might act on the emotional thrill of owning it. But if you pause and reflect, you might realize the real motivation: impressing others or masking insecurity. Awareness helps you align your decision with your true priorities — maybe saving the money for something more meaningful.

Common Pitfalls in Building Awareness

1. Ignoring Early Red Flags:

The first signs of instinct misfiring are subtle. Pay attention to small moments of discomfort or hesitation.

2. Confusing Overthinking with Awareness:

Awareness isn't obsessing over every detail — it's about noticing what matters most.

3. Relying on Awareness Alone:

Awareness is the first step, but it must be paired with action. Recognizing a problem isn't enough; you must address it.

Takeaway

Awareness is your flashlight in the dark, revealing what's influencing your decisions. By pausing, reflecting, and questioning, you gain the clarity to act intentionally rather than react instinctively.

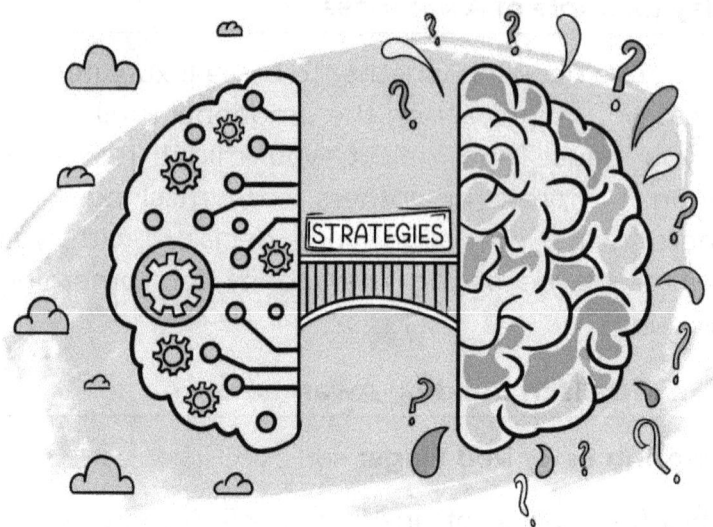

Chapter 6: The AI Advantage

What Makes AI Different?

AI approaches decision-making in ways that human intuition cannot. While humans are influenced by emotions, biases, and limited memory, AI analyzes problems with:

- **Data-Driven Precision:** Every decision is based on evidence, not feelings or assumptions.

- **Pattern Recognition:** AI identifies trends and outcomes that human intuition might miss.

- **Unwavering Objectivity:** It doesn't care about comfort, social pressures, or fear of failure.

This isn't to say humans should think like robots — emotions and intuition have their place. But by adopting certain AI-like strategies, you can overcome instinct's limits and make clearer, more rational choices.

1. Focus on Data, Not Assumptions:

AI gathers as much relevant information as possible before making a decision. Similarly, base your choices on facts, not feelings or guesses.

Example: Before deciding on a business idea, research market demand, competitor analysis, and costs. Don't rely solely on excitement or opinions from friends.

2. Use Probabilities to Weigh Outcomes:

AI calculates the likelihood of different outcomes to guide its choices. You can do the same by asking, "What's the probability of success, failure, or other scenarios?"

Example: When choosing a career switch, consider:

- What's the chance this job aligns with my goals?
- What's the risk of financial instability?
- What's my backup plan?

3. Remove Emotional Noise:

AI isn't swayed by emotions, which helps it stay objective. While you shouldn't ignore emotions, you can set them aside temporarily to evaluate options logically.

4. Test and Adapt:

AI thrives on feedback, adjusting its decisions based on new data. Similarly, treat decisions as experiments. Be ready to pivot if outcomes don't align with your expectations.

Example: If a new habit isn't working (e.g., waking up early to exercise), adjust the approach rather than abandoning the goal.

Everyday Example of Thinking Like AI

Let's say you're deciding whether to rent or buy a home.

- Without an AI approach, you might lean on emotions (buying feels like "success") or assumptions ("Renting is throwing money away").

- With an AI mindset, you'd analyze data: local property values, interest rates, maintenance costs, and your financial goals. This objective evaluation leads to a choice aligned with your circumstances.

Common Pitfalls in Applying AI Thinking

1. Over-Reliance on Data:

Don't ignore emotional or human factors — like relationships or personal values — just because they aren't quantifiable.

2. Analysis Paralysis:

Too much data can delay decisions. Learn to identify the most relevant information.

3. Ignoring Context:

AI is great at analyzing structured problems but less effective at accounting for human nuances like culture, trust, or emotional needs. Balance logic with empathy.

Takeaway

AI-inspired decision-making isn't about abandoning your humanity; it's about using data, probabilities, and logic to balance emotional instincts. By thinking like AI, you can overcome biases, manage risks, and make clearer, more effective choices.

Chapter 7: Decision-Making in the Modern World

Why Modern Life Makes Decisions Harder

In the past, decisions were simpler. Choices were limited, and the risks were often clear: hunt here or there, save food or eat it now. But in today's fast-paced, hyperconnected world, decision-making has become a minefield. You're faced with:

1. Information Overload:

You have access to lots of data, but more information doesn't always mean better decisions. Without focus, too many facts can lead to poor conclusions.

Example: Trying to choose the best insurance plan might involve comparing dozens of policies, leaving you overwhelmed and unsure.

2. Endless Options:

Whether it's picking a career, streaming a movie, or choosing a restaurant, modern life offers limitless choices. Paradoxically, this abundance often makes people less satisfied because they fear missing out on the "perfect" option.

3. Social and Digital Pressures:

Social media amplifies comparisons and expectations. You're bombarded with other people's curated success stories, creating unnecessary pressure to "keep up."

4. Complex Trade-Offs:

Decisions today often involve balancing long-term outcomes with short-term sacrifices. For example, should you prioritize saving for retirement or paying off debt now?

The Impact of Decision Fatigue

Decision fatigue occurs when making too many choices in a short time drains your mental energy. As your brain tires, the quality of your decisions declines. You're more likely to:

- Default to the easiest option (e.g., picking fast food instead of cooking).

- Avoid deciding altogether, postponing action.

- Make impulsive choices to "get it over with."

How to Navigate Modern Challenges

1. Simplify Repetitive Decisions:

Reduce the number of minor choices you make daily by creating routines or rules.

Example: Plan your meals for the week in advance, wear a simple wardrobe, or automate bill payments. This frees mental energy for more significant decisions.

2. Set Boundaries on Information:

Limit how much data you consume. Instead of reading every review, pick two or three reliable sources.

Example: When shopping online, set a time limit for research and stick to it.

3. Prioritize Decisions by Impact:

Not all choices are equally important. Focus your energy on decisions with long-term consequences, and let smaller ones take care of themselves.

Example: Spend time deciding on your career path, but don't overthink what movie to watch tonight.

4. Take Strategic Breaks:

Pause between decisions to recharge your mental energy. A short walk, deep breathing, or stepping away from your screen can improve clarity.

Everyday Example of Modern Decision Challenges

Imagine you're shopping for a new phone.

- Without focus, you might compare 20 models, read 50 reviews, and spend days deliberating.

- With a streamlined approach, you'd narrow your choices to two brands, compare the top features that matter to you, and decide within an hour.

Simplifying the process reduces stress and helps you make confident decisions faster.

Common Pitfalls in Modern Decision-Making

1. FOMO (Fear of Missing Out):

Obsessing over finding the "perfect" choice can lead to indecision or dissatisfaction, even after deciding.

2. Overvaluing Popular Opinion:

Social proof (e.g., product ratings or peer recommendations) is helpful but shouldn't override personal priorities.

3. Relying Too Much on Technology:

Apps and algorithms can assist decisions, but blindly following them can disconnect you from your values and needs.

Takeaway

Modern decision-making is challenging, but it's also full of opportunities. By simplifying choices, focusing on what matters, and managing your mental energy, you can thrive in today's world.

Chapter 8: Defining Success In Decision-making

What Is a "Good Decision"?

Many people define a good decision as one that delivers the desired outcome. But here's the catch: outcomes depend on factors you can't control, like timing, luck, or other people's actions. A decision can be sound even if it doesn't lead to success.

A truly good decision isn't just about results. It's about making a choice that:

1. **Aligns with Your Goals:** Does this move you closer to what you want in life?

2. **Reflects Your Values:** Does this choice respect what's most important to you?

3. Fits Your Circumstances: Does this choice make sense for your current situation?

When a decision aligns with these three elements, it's solid — regardless of the outcome.

How to Define Your Goals, Values, and Circumstances

1. Clarify Your Goals:

Ask, "What am I trying to achieve?" Be specific. For example, "I want to grow my career" is vague, but "I want a role with leadership opportunities" is clear.

2. Identify Your Core Values:

Values are the principles that matter most to you, like integrity, freedom, or family. Decisions that conflict with your values often lead to regret.

Example: If family is a top value, a high-paying job that requires constant travel might not feel like success, even if it looks impressive on paper.

3. Assess Your Circumstances:

Consider your resources, constraints, and timing. A decision that aligns with your goals but ignores your current financial or emotional state might not be realistic.

Practical Example: Defining Success

You're deciding whether to pursue graduate school.

- **Goal:** To advance your career.

- **Value:** Work-life balance.

- **Circumstances:** Limited savings and no desire to relocate.

A "good decision" might involve finding an online or part-time program that fits your budget and lifestyle, rather than enrolling in a costly, full-time course that conflicts with your values or circumstances.

Why Chasing Perfection Is a Trap

Many people equate success with making the "perfect" decision. This mindset leads to overthinking, fear of failure, and dissatisfaction. Remember, good decisions are about *progress,* not perfection.

Common Pitfalls in Defining Success

1. Letting Others Define It for You:

Success looks different for everyone. Don't let societal pressures or family expectations dictate your choices.

2. Over-Focusing on Outcomes:

Even great decisions can lead to disappointing results. Judge the quality of your process, not just the result.

3. Ignoring the Big Picture:

A decision might feel successful in the short term but conflict with your long-term goals.

Takeaway

A good decision is one that reflects your goals, values, and circumstances. When you stop chasing perfection and define success on your own terms, decision-making becomes clearer and more rewarding.

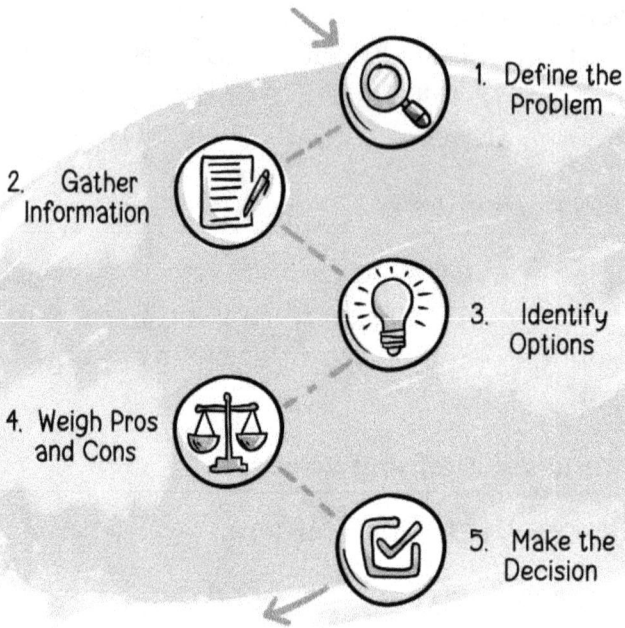

1. Define the Problem
2. Gather Information
3. Identify Options
4. Weigh Pros and Cons
5. Make the Decision

Chapter 9: The Decision-Making Blueprint

Why You Need a Decision-Making Framework

Imagine trying to build a house without a blueprint. Even with the best materials, you'd struggle to create a stable structure. Decision-making is no different. Without a clear framework, your choices risk being haphazard, rushed, or incomplete.

The 5-step blueprint below simplifies the process and ensures you tackle decisions methodically, no matter how complex they seem.

Step 1: Define the Problem

What Are You Really Deciding?

Many poor decisions stem from unclear goals. If you don't know the exact problem you're solving, you're likely to make choices that miss the mark.

Example: Instead of asking, "Should I quit my job?" clarify the real issue: "Do I need a role that offers more growth?" A vague problem leads to vague solutions.

How to Do It:

- Write down the problem in one clear sentence.

- Ask "Why?" until you uncover the root cause.

Step 2: Gather Information

What Do You Need to Know?

Before deciding, gather facts, perspectives, and context. However, avoid falling into the trap of "information overload." You don't need every detail — just the ones that matter most.

Example: If you're deciding whether to buy a house, focus on key factors like location, budget, and long-term value, rather than obsessing over minor details like paint colors.

How to Do It:

- Identify what information is critical to the decision.

- Use trusted sources (data, experts, personal experience).

- Set a time limit for research to avoid paralysis.

Step 3: Identify Options

What Are Your Choices?

List all possible courses of action, even the unconventional ones. People often default to the most obvious options, but creativity can uncover better solutions.

Example: If you're trying to save money, your options might include cutting discretionary spending, finding a side hustle, or relocating to a lower-cost area.

How to Do It:

- Brainstorm without judgment — write down every option, no matter how impractical it seems.

- Narrow your list to realistic, actionable choices.

Step 4: Weigh Pros and Cons

What Are the Trade-Offs?

Every decision has benefits and downsides. Understanding these trade-offs helps you make an informed choice. Consider both short-term and long-term impacts.

Example: When deciding whether to take a promotion, weigh the pros (higher pay, new challenges) against the cons (longer hours, more stress).

How to Do It:

- Create a table with two columns: Pros and Cons.

- Assign each factor a weight based on its importance.

- Pay special attention to deal-breakers, like misalignment with your values or goals.

Step 5: Make the Decision

What's Your Final Choice?

This is where you act. Once you've analyzed the options, pick the one that best aligns with your goals, values, and circumstances. Avoid lingering in indecision.

Example: After weighing the pros and cons of taking the promotion, you decide it aligns with your career goals despite the longer hours.

How to Do It:

- Trust the process. If you've followed the steps, your decision is likely sound.

- Commit to your choice. Second-guessing only wastes time and creates anxiety.

Practical Example: Using the Blueprint

You're deciding whether to go back to school.

1. **Define the Problem:** "Do I need additional education to advance my career?"

2. **Gather Information:** Research programs, costs, and time commitments.

3. **Identify Options:** Full-time enrollment, part-time classes, or self-study.

4. **Weigh Pros and Cons:** Compare benefits like career growth with downsides like debt or time away from family.

5. **Make the Decision:** Choose the path that aligns with your goals and circumstances.

Common Pitfalls in Decision Frameworks

1. **Skipping Steps:** Jumping straight to action without clarifying the problem or weighing options.

2. **Perfectionism:** Waiting for a "perfect" solution before deciding.

3. **Failure to Act:** Overanalyzing until the opportunity passes.

Takeaway

The decision-making blueprint is a simple, repeatable process that works for decisions big and small. By following these five steps, you'll reduce uncertainty, minimize regret, and make choices with confidence.

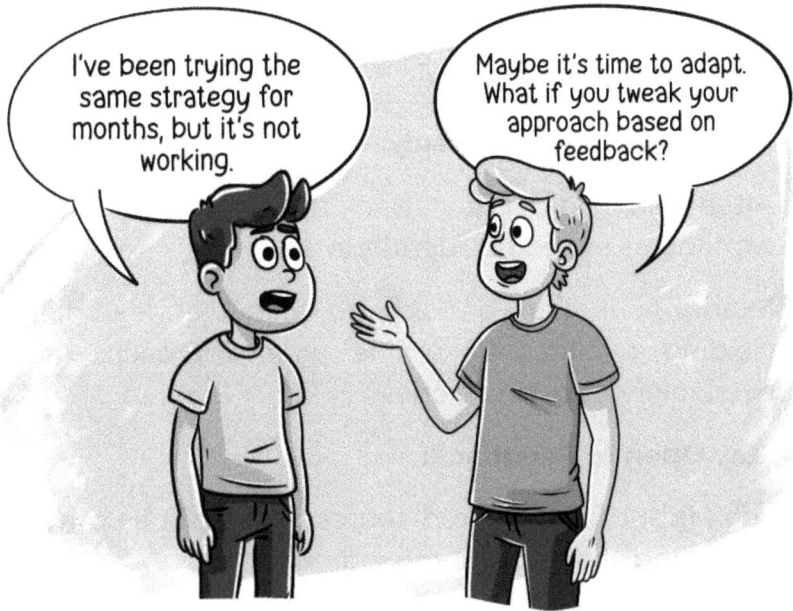

Chapter 10: Adaptability Matters

Why Adaptability Is Essential

Even the best decision-making strategies can't predict every variable. Circumstances change, outcomes surprise you, and new information emerges. Adaptability is the ability to adjust your approach when the unexpected happens, ensuring that you stay on track even when the path shifts.

How Rigidity Fails You

Rigid thinkers stick to a plan even when it's no longer working. This "sunk cost" mindset can trap you in poor decisions because you're afraid to pivot.

Example: Imagine you've started a business, but sales are falling flat. A rigid thinker might keep pouring money into the original strategy, hoping things will improve. An adaptable thinker would analyze why it's not working and consider pivoting to a new product or approach.

How to Develop Adaptability

1. Monitor Outcomes Closely:

After making a decision, track the results. If things aren't working as expected, identify why.

Example: If your decision to follow a new diet isn't yielding results, re-examine your approach. Are you overlooking hidden calories?

2. Stay Open to Feedback:

Seek input from trusted sources. Sometimes others can spot blind spots you've missed.

Example: A mentor or colleague might suggest a different approach to solving a work problem, one you hadn't considered.

3. Be Willing to Let Go:

If a decision isn't working, don't cling to it out of pride or fear. Adjust your course as needed.

Example: If a career move doesn't align with your happiness, it's okay to rethink your path and pivot to something more fulfilling.

4. Plan for Flexibility:

Build adaptability into your decisions. For example, when setting a financial goal, leave room for unexpected expenses.

Everyday Example of Adaptability

You decide to move to a new city for a job, but after six months, you realize the role doesn't align with your career goals. Instead of forcing yourself to stay, you explore new opportunities in the city or consider returning home. Adaptability lets you turn a disappointing outcome into a stepping stone for growth.

Common Pitfalls in Adaptability

1. **Fear of Change:** Sticking to a decision because changing course feels like failure.

2. **Over-Correcting:** Constantly shifting plans without giving them time to work.

3. **Ignoring Feedback:** Refusing to adjust because you're too attached to the original choice.

Takeaway

Adaptability is your safety net in a world of uncertainty. No strategy guarantees success, but the ability to adjust ensures you can thrive no matter what life throws your way.

With the foundations of decision-making now in place, you're ready to explore advanced strategies that sharpen your thinking even further.

Part II: Mental Models for Superior Thinking

This section focuses on mental models that drive personal and professional growth. These models are the key to lifelong growth, making progress manageable and meaningful.

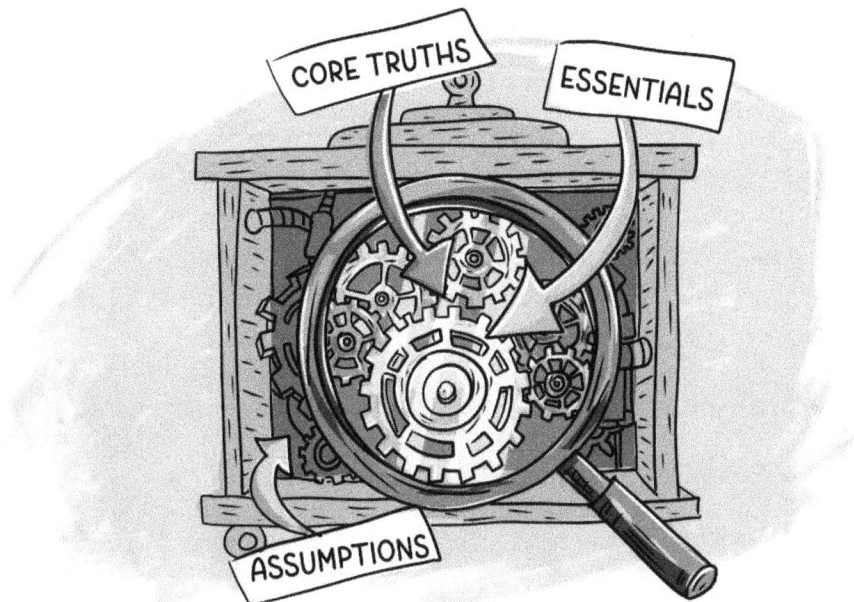

Chapter 11: First Principles Thinking

What Is First Principles Thinking?

First Principles Thinking is about drilling down to the core of a problem, stripping away all assumptions, and identifying the fundamental building blocks. Instead of solving problems by tweaking what already exists, this approach starts from scratch, asking, "What do we *know* to be true?"

Example:

If you want to make transportation faster, most people might assume "improving the car" is the answer. But First Principles Thinking breaks it down: What's the goal? To move from point A to B quickly. What's essential? Speed, energy, and safety. By challenging the assumption that cars are necessary, you open the door to innovations like high-speed rail or hyperloop systems.

Why First Principles Thinking Matters

Traditional problem-solving relies on analogies — looking at what others have done and iterating on it. While useful, it can trap you in conventional thinking. First Principles Thinking lets you question "the way things have always been done" and uncover innovative solutions.

Benefits Include:

- Breaking free from outdated assumptions.

- Unlocking creativity and innovation.

- Creating solutions tailored to your goals, not past models.

How to Use First Principles Thinking

1. Identify Assumptions:

List everything you believe about the problem, even things that seem "obvious." Many assumptions are hidden in plain sight.

Example: If you're starting a business, you might assume, "I need a physical office."

Challenge this: Is that truly necessary, or could a remote setup work better?

2. Ask "Why?" Until You Can't Anymore:

Like peeling an onion, keep asking "Why?" until you reach truths that are undeniable and cannot be simplified further.

Example: If you assume "I need money to succeed," ask why. Maybe what you truly need is resources or connections, which can be achieved in other ways.

3. Rebuild from Core Truths:

Once you identify the essentials, construct solutions based on them.

Example: If you know a car's purpose is to move people efficiently, consider whether alternative materials, shapes, or energy sources could better serve that goal.

Practical Example: Saving Money

Instead of following generic advice like "stop buying coffee," First Principles Thinking asks:

- Why am I overspending? (I buy takeout.)

- Why do I buy takeout? (I don't plan meals.)

- Why don't I plan meals? (I lack time or energy.)

The core problem isn't coffee; it's poor planning. Solving that — by prepping meals in advance — has a greater impact.

Common Pitfalls in First Principles Thinking

1. Stopping Too Soon:

You might think you've reached the root when you're still operating on assumptions. Dig deeper.

2. Mistaking Assumptions for Truths:

Not everything you think is fundamental truly is. Challenge every belief until it's proven indispensable.

3. Overcomplicating:

Focus on the essentials. Don't get bogged down in irrelevant details.

Takeaway

First Principles Thinking transforms how you approach problems. By breaking issues down to their core truths and rebuilding from there, you open the door to solutions others never see.

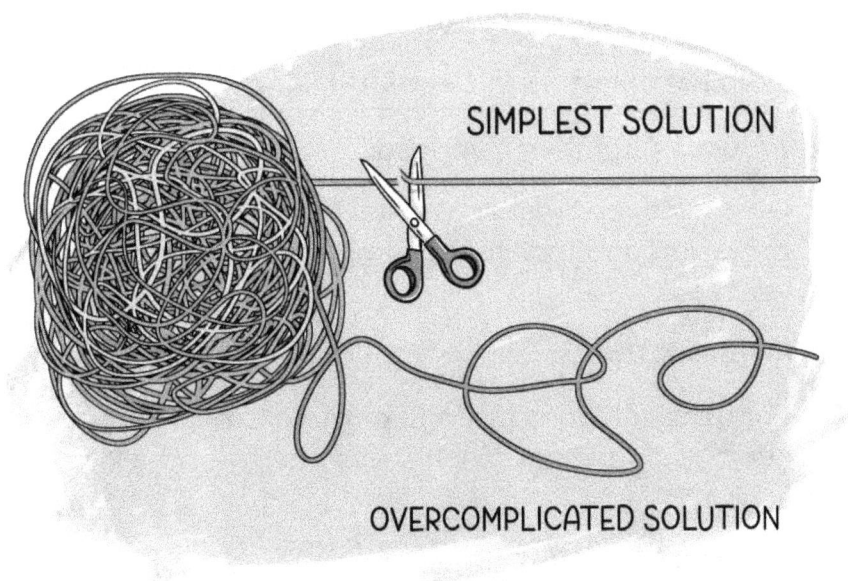

SIMPLEST SOLUTION

OVERCOMPLICATED SOLUTION

Chapter 12: Occam's Razor

What Is Occam's Razor?

Occam's Razor says: "The simplest solution is often the best." When faced with multiple explanations, favor the one that requires the fewest assumptions. This doesn't mean the simplest answer is *always* correct — just that it's the best starting point until more evidence suggests otherwise.

Example:

You wake up to find your car won't start.

- Overcomplicated Thinking: "It must be a rare engine defect caused by a specific manufacturing error."

- Occam's Razor: "The battery is probably dead."

By focusing on the most straightforward explanation, you avoid wasting time and energy on unnecessary possibilities.

Why Simplicity Matters in Decision-Making

1. Reduces Cognitive Overload:

Overthinking creates mental clutter, which leads to confusion and indecision. Simplifying the problem helps you focus.

2. Increases Efficiency:

Complex solutions often take more time, resources, and effort. A simple approach saves energy and allows faster action.

3. Improves Clarity:

A clear, simple solution is easier to communicate and execute.

How to Apply Occam's Razor

1. Identify the Core Problem:

Strip away distractions and pinpoint the central issue.

Example: If your team is missing deadlines, don't immediately assume it's due to poor management or complex workflows. Start by asking: "Are there too many tasks assigned to too few people?"

2. List Possible Explanations or Solutions:

Write down all the options, from the simplest to the most complex.

Example: If your internet is slow, explanations could range from "router issues" (simple) to "interference from local construction" (complex).

3. Choose the Simplest Option First:

Test the easiest explanation or solution before exploring more complicated ones.

Everyday Example of Occam's Razor

You're deciding whether to buy a new laptop.

- Overcomplicated: Research 10 different brands, compare endless reviews, and worry about features you'll never use.

- Simple: Focus on your primary need (e.g., work or school) and choose a reliable, budget-friendly model that meets those needs.

Common Pitfalls in Using Occam's Razor

1. Oversimplifying:

The simplest solution isn't *always* correct. Use evidence to confirm it before committing.

2. Ignoring Nuances:

While simplicity is valuable, don't disregard important details just to make a decision faster.

3. Rushing to Conclusions:

Don't confuse "simple" with "quick." Take time to evaluate before acting.

Takeaway

Occam's Razor cuts through complexity to reveal clarity. Start with the simplest explanation or solution, but stay open to new evidence. Simplifying your thinking doesn't just save time — it leads to smarter, more efficient decisions.

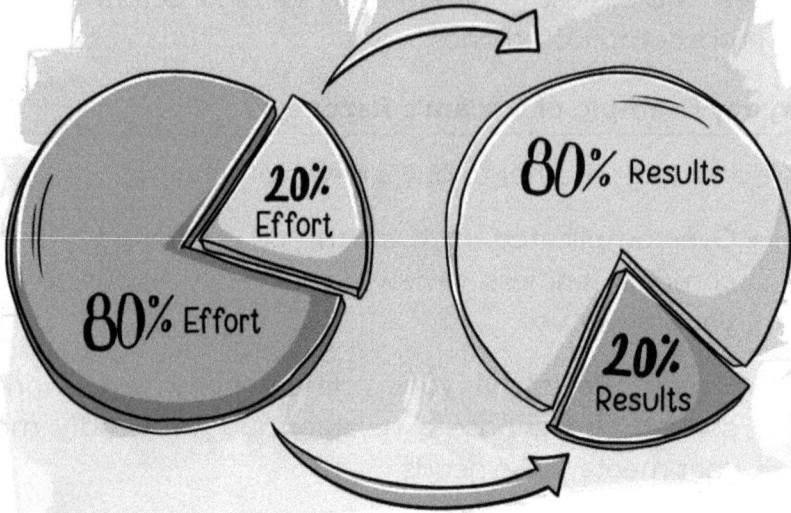

Chapter 13: The Pareto Principle

What Is the Pareto Principle?

Also called the "80/20 Rule," the Pareto Principle states that 80% of outcomes come from 20% of efforts. This idea is found everywhere:

- 80% of a company's revenue often comes from 20% of its clients.

- 80% of results in a workout might come from 20% of the exercises.

- 80% of your stress may come from just 20% of your responsibilities.

By focusing on the "vital few" (the 20% that matters), you can maximize results with less effort.

Why the Pareto Principle Matters in Decision-Making

1. Prioritizes Impact:

Helps you identify and focus on high-impact activities rather than spreading yourself too thin.

2. Eliminates Waste:

Avoids wasting time, money, and energy on low-value tasks.

3. Improves Productivity:

Shifting your focus to the most effective efforts makes your work more efficient.

How to Apply the Pareto Principle

1. Identify the Vital Few:

Ask, "Which 20% of my actions, clients, or tasks are creating 80% of my results?"

Example: If you're studying, focus on the 20% of topics that will appear most frequently on the test.

2. Eliminate or Minimize the Trivial Many:

Once you know what doesn't contribute much, spend less time or energy on those activities.

Example: At work, stop micromanaging minor tasks and delegate them, so you can focus on strategic priorities.

3. Redistribute Resources:

Shift your time, money, and attention to the high-impact 20%.

Example: If 20% of your marketing campaigns generate 80% of your sales, invest more in those campaigns and scale back the rest.

Everyday Example of the Pareto Principle

Let's say you're cleaning your house. Instead of deep-cleaning every corner, focus on the 20% of areas (like the kitchen and living room) where 80% of clutter accumulates. This approach gives you the biggest improvement with the least effort.

Common Pitfalls in Applying the Pareto Principle

1. Misidentifying the 20%:

Be careful not to assume — use evidence or data to determine what's truly high-impact.

2. Neglecting the Long Tail:

While the 80% may not produce as much value, it's often necessary for long-term success. Don't ignore it entirely.

3. Over-Simplifying:

Not everything follows the 80/20 split perfectly. Treat it as a guideline, not a hard rule.

Takeaway

The Pareto Principle is a tool for prioritization. By identifying and focusing on the 20% of actions that drive 80% of the results, you'll achieve more with less effort. But remember — the real skill lies in knowing what matters most.

Chapter 14: Second-Order Thinking

What Is Second-Order Thinking?

Second-Order Thinking is the art of looking beyond the obvious. While most people stop at the immediate impact of a decision (first-order thinking), second-order thinkers anticipate the ripple effects — the long-term and indirect consequences that follow. This approach doesn't just solve problems; it helps avoid creating new ones.

Example:

Suppose a company decides to cut costs by reducing employee benefits. The first-order effect is clear: lower expenses. But second-order thinking reveals the hidden costs: reduced employee morale, higher turnover rates, and difficulty attracting top talent.

Instead of stopping at "What happens now?" Second-Order Thinking asks, "And then what?"

Why Second-Order Thinking Matters

1. Avoids Unintended Consequences:

Short-sighted decisions often create bigger problems down the line. Second-Order Thinking helps you anticipate these outcomes and adjust your strategy.

2. Reveals Hidden Opportunities:

Long-term effects aren't always negative. Thinking deeper can uncover positive ripple effects that others miss.

3. Gives You a Strategic Edge:

Most people focus on immediate outcomes. Second-order thinkers see the bigger picture, making more informed and resilient choices.

How to Practice Second-Order Thinking

1. List the Immediate Impact (First-Order Effect):

Start with the obvious. Ask, "What's the direct result of this decision?"

Example: You decide to offer a discount to attract customers. The first-order effect is increased sales.

2. Ask "What Happens Next?" (Second-Order Effects):

Consider the next layer of consequences.

Example: The discount might attract bargain hunters who don't become loyal customers, reducing your overall profitability.

3. Go Deeper (Third-Order Effects):

Keep asking, "And then what?" until you've mapped out the longer-term consequences.

Example: Competitors might feel pressured to lower their prices in response, triggering a price war that hurts the entire industry.

4. Weigh the Trade-Offs:

Once you've mapped out the ripple effects, evaluate whether the long-term benefits outweigh the risks.

Example: If the short-term sales boost leads to brand devaluation, the discount strategy might not be worth it.

Everyday Example of Second-Order Thinking

Imagine you're deciding whether to stay up late binge-watching a show.

- **First-Order Effect:** You enjoy the entertainment.

- **Second-Order Effect:** You wake up tired, reducing your productivity the next day.

- **Third-Order Effect:** Poor performance at work might impact your reputation, causing stress or missed opportunities.

By thinking beyond the immediate gratification, you might decide to save the binge for the weekend instead.

Common Pitfalls in Second-Order Thinking

1. Stopping at the First Ripple:

Many people make decisions based only on immediate results, ignoring the long-term picture.

2. Overlooking Complexity:

Not every ripple is predictable. Be prepared for surprises and adjust as new information emerges.

3. Focusing Only on Negatives:

While second-order thinking often highlights risks, don't forget to look for hidden benefits.

Takeaway

Second-Order Thinking forces you to see decisions as part of a larger chain of events. By anticipating ripple effects, you can avoid short-sighted mistakes and make choices that hold up over time.

Now that you're thinking beyond the immediate, let's explore a powerful mental tool for creative problem-solving.

Work Backward to Move Forward.

Chapter 15: Inversion

What Is Inversion?

Inversion is a problem-solving technique that flips the script. Instead of asking, "How do I achieve this?" you ask, "What could prevent me from achieving this?" By identifying obstacles or worst-case scenarios first, you gain clarity on how to avoid failure and achieve success.

Example:

Instead of asking, "How can I be happy?" invert the question: "What makes people unhappy, and how can I avoid those things?"

This reverse approach often reveals insights that traditional thinking misses.

Why Inversion Works

1. Clarifies the Problem:

Focusing on what could go wrong helps you see the problem more clearly.

2. Uncovers Hidden Obstacles:

Anticipating failure points makes it easier to address them before they happen.

3. Simplifies Complex Problems:

Working backward breaks big challenges into manageable steps.

How to Apply Inversion

1. State Your Goal:

Start with the problem you're trying to solve.

Example: "How can I build a successful career?"

2. Invert the Question:

Ask, "What would guarantee failure?"

Example: "What habits or actions would ruin my career?"

3. Identify Failure Points:

List the factors that would lead to the worst-case scenario.

Example: Missing deadlines, neglecting skill development, or burning bridges with colleagues.

4. Work Backward:

Plan strategies to avoid those failure points.

Example: Create a schedule to meet deadlines, commit to lifelong learning, and focus on building strong relationships at work.

Everyday Example of Inversion

Imagine you're planning a road trip.

- **Normal Thinking:** "How can I make this trip great?"
- **Inverted Thinking:** "What could ruin the trip?"

The inverted approach might reveal risks like car trouble, bad weather, or forgetting essential items. Addressing these risks in advance — by servicing your car, checking the forecast, and packing carefully — ensures a smoother trip.

Common Pitfalls in Inversion

1. Getting Stuck in Negatives:

While identifying risks is useful, don't focus so much on failure that you lose sight of success.

2. Overlooking Small Obstacles:

Minor issues (e.g., procrastination or poor communication) can derail progress just as much as major ones.

3. Failing to Take Action:

Recognizing potential problems is only helpful if you act to prevent them.

Takeaway

Inversion flips your perspective, helping you solve problems by working backward. By identifying and avoiding failure points, you clear the path to success.

Chapter 16: Opportunity Cost

What Is Opportunity Cost?

Every decision comes with a trade-off: choosing one option means giving up another. Opportunity cost is the value of the choice you *didn't* make. It's not just about money; it's about time, energy, and the potential outcomes you could have pursued instead.

Example:

Imagine you spend $1,000 on a vacation. The opportunity cost isn't just the money — it's also the investment or savings you could have made with that same amount, or even the skill you could have learned during that time.

Why Opportunity Cost Matters

1. Reveals Hidden Trade-Offs:

Many choices feel "free" because you don't immediately see what you're giving up. Opportunity cost forces you to think about what you're sacrificing.

2. Improves Resource Allocation:

By understanding what's at stake, you can better allocate your time, money, and energy to what matters most.

3. Sharpens Priorities:

Opportunity cost helps you focus on the activities and decisions that align with your long-term goals.

How to Evaluate Opportunity Cost

1. Clarify Your Resources:

Identify the time, money, or energy each option will require.

Example: If you're deciding between two job offers, consider not just the salary but also the commute, work-life balance, and career growth potential.

2. Ask "What Else Could I Be Doing?"

Think about the alternatives you're giving up by choosing this option.

Example: If you choose to spend your weekend binge-watching TV, the opportunity cost might be the gym session or quality time with loved ones you could have enjoyed instead.

3. Compare the Long-Term Value:

Focus on the future. Which option offers the greatest long-term benefits?

Example: Spending money on a flashy gadget might feel good now, but investing that money in stocks could grow your wealth over time.

Everyday Example of Opportunity Cost

Imagine you're deciding whether to buy a new car.

- **The Obvious Cost:** The car's price and maintenance.

- **The Opportunity Cost:** The vacation, savings, or home improvements you could have spent that money on instead.

By considering what you're giving up, you can make a more thoughtful decision.

Common Pitfalls in Evaluating Opportunity Cost

1. Overlooking Intangible Costs:

Sometimes, the cost isn't financial — it's emotional or social, like missing out on time with family.

2. Underestimating Time:

People often forget that time is a finite resource. Spending an hour on one activity means losing an hour for something else.

3. Paralysis by Analysis:

Thinking too much about opportunity cost can lead to indecision. Use it as a guide, not a roadblock.

Takeaway

Opportunity cost is the invisible price tag of every choice. By considering what you're giving up, you'll make decisions that align with your values and maximize your resources.

	URGENT	NOT URGENT
IMPORTANT	(alarm clock)	(calendar 31)
NOT IMPORTANT	(phone ringing)	(remote control)

Chapter 17: The Eisenhower Matrix

What Is the Eisenhower Matrix?

The Eisenhower Matrix is a decision-making tool that helps you prioritize tasks by urgency and importance. Named after U.S. President Dwight D. Eisenhower, it's based on his principle: "What is important is seldom urgent, and what is urgent is seldom important."

The matrix divides tasks into four categories:

1. **Important & Urgent:** Tasks that need immediate action.

2. **Important but Not Urgent:** Tasks that require planning and long-term focus.

3. **Not Important but Urgent:** Tasks that feel pressing but don't contribute to your goals.

4. Not Important & Not Urgent: Distractions to eliminate or minimize.

Why the Eisenhower Matrix Matters

1. Prevents Overwhelm:

Helps you focus on what truly matters instead of getting lost in busywork.

2. Improves Time Management:

Ensures your energy goes to high-priority tasks rather than low-value activities.

3. Encourages Long-Term Thinking:

Keeps you focused on goals rather than reactive to daily demands.

How to Use the Eisenhower Matrix

1. List Your Tasks:

Write down everything you need to do, no matter how small.

2. Categorize by Importance and Urgency:

Place each task into one of the four quadrants.

Example:

- o A looming project deadline? Important & Urgent.

- o Planning a career move? Important but Not Urgent.

- o Responding to a non-critical email? Not Important but Urgent.

3. Act Accordingly:

- o **Important & Urgent:** Do these tasks immediately.

- o **Important but Not Urgent:** Schedule them for later and protect the time.

- o **Not Important but Urgent:** Delegate if possible.

- o **Not Important & Not Urgent:** Eliminate or minimize.

Everyday Example of the Eisenhower Matrix

You're planning your day and have the following tasks:

1. **Prepare a report due today (Important & Urgent).**

2. **Exercise for health (Important but Not Urgent).**

3. **Answer an email about a minor issue (Not Important but Urgent).**

4. **Scroll social media (Not Important & Not Urgent).**

The matrix helps you prioritize the report, schedule exercise, delegate the email, and avoid social media altogether.

Common Pitfalls in Using the Eisenhower Matrix

1. Misjudging Importance:

Not everything urgent is important. Learn to distinguish between real priorities and busywork.

2. Failing to Delegate:

You don't have to do everything yourself. Delegate low-value tasks when possible.

3. Ignoring the "Not Urgent" Quadrant:

Long-term goals often fall into the "Important but Not Urgent" category. Don't neglect them.

Takeaway

The Eisenhower Matrix is your roadmap to smarter prioritization. By categorizing tasks and acting strategically, you'll manage your time effectively and stay focused on what matters most.

Chapter 18: Bayesian Thinking

What Is Bayesian Thinking?

Bayesian Thinking is a decision-making framework rooted in flexibility. Named after the mathematician Thomas Bayes, it's about updating your beliefs and decisions as new evidence emerges. Instead of sticking rigidly to what you *think* is true, Bayesian Thinking asks:

- **What do I currently believe?**

- **What new evidence do I have?**

- **How should this evidence adjust my belief?**

Example:

Imagine you assume it will rain because the sky looks cloudy. Then, you check the weather forecast, which shows a 10%

chance of rain. Bayesian Thinking encourages you to update your belief based on the forecast and carry an umbrella only if it makes sense in the context.

Why Bayesian Thinking Matters

1. Promotes Adaptability:

It helps you pivot your decisions when circumstances change.

2. Reduces Stubbornness:

Humans tend to cling to old beliefs, even when presented with contrary evidence. Bayesian Thinking combats this bias.

3. Encourages Rationality:

Decisions become less about guesswork and more about weighing probabilities.

How to Apply Bayesian Thinking

1. Start with a Baseline Belief:

Begin with your initial assumption or "best guess."

Example: You believe a business idea has a 70% chance of success based on past experience.

2. Incorporate New Evidence:

When new data arrives, evaluate its reliability and relevance.

Example: A market report shows declining interest in your target product.

3. Adjust Your Belief:

Update your probability based on the strength of the evidence.

Example: After reviewing the report, you lower the success probability of your idea to 50% and decide to adjust your strategy.

4. Act Based on Updated Beliefs:

Use your revised perspective to guide your next steps.

Example: Pivot to a different market segment where demand is stronger.

Everyday Example of Bayesian Thinking

Imagine you're hiring a candidate.

- **Baseline Belief:** Based on their résumé, you assume they're highly qualified.

- **New Evidence:** During the interview, they struggle to answer key technical questions.

- **Updated Belief:** You revise your assumption, concluding they may lack certain skills.

- **Action:** You decide to evaluate other candidates before making a final decision.

Common Pitfalls in Bayesian Thinking

1. Ignoring Evidence:

People often dismiss new data if it conflicts with their existing beliefs.

2. Overreacting to Weak Evidence:

Not all new information is reliable. Evaluate the quality of the evidence before adjusting your belief.

3. Failing to Act on Updated Beliefs:

Even if you revise your perspective, it's meaningless if you don't adapt your decisions accordingly.

Takeaway

Bayesian Thinking teaches you to view decisions as dynamic, not static. By continuously updating your beliefs with new evidence, you stay flexible and make choices grounded in reality.

Chapter 19: Regret Minimization

What Is Regret Minimization?

Regret Minimization is a decision-making strategy that prioritizes long-term peace of mind over short-term comfort. Instead of asking, "What's easiest right now?" it asks:

- **What choice will I regret the least in 10 years?**

- **How will I feel about this decision when I look back on it later?**

Example:

You're deciding whether to take a leap and start your own business. In the short term, staying at your current job feels safer. But through the lens of regret minimization, you might realize you'd regret not trying more than the temporary risks of failure.

Why Regret Minimization Matters

1. Keeps You Focused on the Big Picture:

It helps you prioritize meaningful goals over fleeting emotions or convenience.

2. Combats Decision Paralysis:

Thinking long-term clarifies what truly matters, making tough decisions easier.

3. Reduces Future Regrets:

By imagining yourself in the future, you can align your decisions with what you'll value most later.

How to Minimize Regret in Decisions

1. Visualize Your Future Self:

Imagine looking back on this decision in 5, 10, or even 20 years. Ask, "What choice will I feel proud of?"

Example: Will skipping a once-in-a-lifetime travel opportunity for work feel like the right decision in 10 years?

2. Weigh Regret vs. Risk:

Sometimes, avoiding short-term discomfort leads to long-term regret. Balance the risks of failure against the regret of never trying.

Example: Starting a side hustle might fail, but the regret of not pursuing your dream might be greater.

3. Focus on What You Can Control:

Regret often comes from fixating on what you can't change. Make the best decision possible with the information you have now.

Everyday Example of Regret Minimization

You're deciding whether to attend a family reunion.

- Short-term: It feels inconvenient and expensive.

- Long-term: You realize you'd regret missing the chance to spend time with loved ones who may not be around forever.

Through regret minimization, you prioritize the experience over temporary discomfort.

Common Pitfalls in Regret Minimization

1. Overthinking Small Choices:

Not every decision needs this level of analysis. Use regret minimization for significant, life-impacting choices.

2. Assuming the Worst:

Don't let fear of regret lead to overly cautious decisions. Focus on what aligns with your values.

3. Neglecting Present Needs:

While thinking long-term is important, don't ignore the short-term realities that affect your well-being.

Takeaway

Regret Minimization puts your future self in the driver's seat, helping you make decisions you'll look back on with pride, not regret.

How many coffee cups are used in this city every day?

Let's break it down: How many people live here? How many drink coffee? And how many cups do they have daily?

Population = 1,000,000
Coffee Drinkers = 50%
(500,000)
Cups per Person = 1.5
Final Estimate = 750,000 cups/day.

Chapter 20: The Fermi Approach

What Is the Fermi Approach?

The Fermi Approach is a practical method for solving problems that seem impossible to measure. Named after the physicist Enrico Fermi, who was famous for making remarkably accurate estimates with limited data, this approach breaks a problem into smaller, manageable pieces.

Instead of waiting for perfect data, you make logical assumptions and build an answer step by step. It's not about being perfectly accurate — it's about being *reasonable enough* to make informed decisions.

Why the Fermi Approach Works

1. Simplifies Complexity:

Big, vague questions become solvable when broken into smaller components.

2. Encourages Logical Thinking:

By focusing on logic instead of guesswork, you create a structured path to clarity.

3. Builds Confidence in Uncertainty:

Instead of being paralyzed by a lack of data, you can still move forward with informed estimates.

How to Apply the Fermi Approach

1. Define the Problem Clearly:

Start with a big question, like "How many coffee cups are sold in my city each day?"

2. Break It Down Into Smaller Questions:

Divide the problem into manageable parts that are easier to estimate. For example:

- How many people live in your city?

- What percentage drink coffee?

- How many cups does each coffee drinker buy daily?

3. Estimate Each Piece:

Make logical, evidence-based guesses for each component.

4. Example:

- City population: 1,000,000 people.

- Percentage of coffee drinkers: 50% (500,000).

- Average cups per drinker: 1.5.

5. Combine Your Estimates:

Multiply or add your answers to reach a final estimate.

Example: 500,000 coffee drinkers × 1.5 cups = 750,000 cups sold daily.

6. Adjust as Needed:

If you get new information or realize a component is off, refine your assumptions and recalculate.

Why the Fermi Approach Is Valuable

The Fermi Approach is useful in situations where:

- You lack complete data but still need an answer.
- Precision isn't critical, but logic and reason are.
- You want to develop a deeper understanding of a complex problem.

Example:

If you're organizing an event, you might need to estimate attendance without knowing exact RSVP numbers. By using logical steps (e.g., how many invitees typically attend such events), you can prepare confidently.

Everyday Example of the Fermi Approach

Question: How much water does your household use in a week?

- **Step 1:** How many people live in your house? (4 people)
- **Step 2:** How much water does one person use daily for drinking, cooking, cleaning, and bathing? (80 gallons per person)
- **Step 3:** Multiply by 7 days.

Estimate: 4 people × 80 gallons × 7 days = 2,240 gallons per week.

While the exact number might vary, this estimate is reasonable enough to plan for water usage or compare with your water bill.

Common Pitfalls in the Fermi Approach

1. Overcomplicating the Problem:

Keep the steps simple. If a component seems too complex, break it into even smaller pieces.

2. Guessing Without Logic:

Assumptions should be based on prior knowledge, averages, or reasonable comparisons, not random guesses.

3. Ignoring Margins of Error:

Acknowledge that your estimate isn't perfect. Build in a margin of error to account for uncertainties.

How the Fermi Approach Boosts Decision-Making

Let's say you're pitching a new business idea: selling reusable water bottles. A key question might be, "How many bottles could we sell in the first year?"

Instead of waiting for expensive market research, apply the Fermi Approach:

1. How many people in your target region? (500,000)

2. What percentage care about sustainability? (30% = 150,000)

3. How many of them might buy a reusable bottle in a year? (10% = 15,000)

Using logical steps, you estimate 15,000 potential buyers —
enough to justify moving forward with your idea.

Takeaway

The Fermi Approach transforms intimidating, unmeasurable
problems into solvable puzzles. By breaking questions into
smaller components, making logical estimates, and combining
them systematically, you can tackle uncertainty with
confidence and clarity.

With this method, you don't need perfect data to make smart
decisions — just a structured approach and a willingness to
think critically.

Part III: Strategies to Overcome Cognitive Biases

In the next ten chapters, I will teach you about tools to help you make smarter, more confident decisions. From planning for the short term to preparing for long-term success, these strategies are easy to apply in everyday life.

Chapter 21: Anchoring Bias

What Is Anchoring Bias?

Anchoring Bias happens when your decisions are overly influenced by the first piece of information you encounter — the "anchor." Even if this anchor is irrelevant or misleading, it can skew your thinking and limit your ability to consider other perspectives.

Anchors come in many forms:

- A high starting price in a negotiation.

- The first opinion you hear on a topic.

- The initial estimate for how long a project will take.

For example, imagine you're shopping for a jacket, and the first one you see is $400. Even if you later see one priced at $200, you might think it's a bargain — not because it's objectively cheap, but because your mind is still tethered to that $400 anchor.

Why Anchoring Bias Matters

Anchoring isn't just a psychological quirk — it has real consequences:

1. **Distorts Judgments:** Anchors warp how you assess value, probability, or time.

2. **Influences Negotiations:** The first number thrown out in a negotiation often dictates the entire range of discussion.

3. **Limits Creativity:** Anchors make it harder to explore alternative options because you keep circling back to that initial idea.

Example in Action:

In a salary negotiation, if an employer offers a low starting figure, you might feel stuck negotiating within that range — even if the role's value justifies a higher salary.

How to Break Free from Anchoring Bias

1. Recognize the Anchor:

Pause and ask yourself: "Is my judgment being influenced by this initial number or idea?" Awareness is the first step to escaping the anchor's pull.

Example: If you're house-hunting and the first home you see is overpriced, recognize that it's setting an artificial standard for what "reasonable" looks like.

2. Do Independent Research:

Gather objective data from multiple sources to counteract the anchor's influence.

Example: Instead of letting the asking price of a car guide you, look up its fair market value to create your own benchmark.

3. Set Your Own Anchors:

Enter decisions with a clear idea of what you believe is reasonable before external anchors can influence you.

Example: Before negotiating a salary, research typical pay for the role and determine your ideal range in advance.

4. Delay Snap Judgments:

Give yourself time to reflect, especially for high-stakes decisions. This helps you reset your perspective and avoid acting impulsively.

Example: If a salesperson pressures you with a "limited-time offer," step back to evaluate if the deal truly aligns with your needs.

Everyday Example of Anchoring Bias

Imagine you're buying groceries. You see a bottle of olive oil priced at $25, and the next one is $15. Even though $15 might still be overpriced, it feels cheap compared to the $25 anchor. Breaking free means asking: "What's the typical price for olive oil?" instead of relying on comparisons to set your judgment.

Common Pitfalls When Addressing Anchoring Bias

1. Failing to Question the Anchor:

Many anchors feel natural, so you might not realize how much they're influencing you.

2. Overvaluing First Impressions:

People often assume that the first number or idea they encounter is accurate, even without evidence.

3. Rushing Decisions:

Anchors are especially powerful under time pressure. Take a moment to pause and evaluate.

Takeaway

Anchoring Bias can tether you to misleading information, clouding your decisions. By identifying anchors, seeking independent data, and setting your own benchmarks, you can think more clearly and break free from the weight of first impressions.

REMOVE THE BLINDERS

Chapter 22: Confirmation Bias

What Is Confirmation Bias?

Confirmation Bias is your brain's tendency to search for, interpret, and prioritize information that supports your existing beliefs while ignoring or dismissing evidence that contradicts them.

It feels good to have your opinions validated — it's comforting and requires less mental effort than rethinking your perspective. But this bias can lead to poor decisions by narrowing your view of the world.

Example:

If you believe that a particular investment is a good idea, you might actively seek out success stories about similar investments while ignoring reports of failures. As a result, you make a decision based on incomplete or one-sided information.

Why Confirmation Bias Matters

1. Distorts Reality:

When you only focus on information that confirms your beliefs, you fail to see the bigger picture.

2. Stifles Growth:

If you're unwilling to consider opposing views, you miss opportunities to learn, improve, or adapt.

3. Reinforces Bad Decisions:

By ignoring critical evidence, you're more likely to double down on flawed choices.

Real-Life Impact:

Imagine a manager who believes their team is performing well. They might only pay attention to positive feedback and ignore warning signs of dissatisfaction, leading to higher turnover.

How to Overcome Confirmation Bias

1. Actively Seek Contradictory Evidence:

Instead of asking, "What supports my belief?" ask, "What challenges it?"

Example: If you believe a certain diet is the best, research studies that critique it instead of just reading testimonials from fans.

2. Engage with Opposing Views:

Talk to people who disagree with you and genuinely try to understand their perspective.

Example: If you're convinced one political policy is ideal, discuss it with someone who supports an alternative to broaden your understanding.

3. Use Neutral Sources:

Rely on objective, unbiased information rather than sources designed to confirm a specific agenda.

Example: Instead of trusting a company's marketing materials, read independent reviews to get a balanced perspective.

4. Ask Disconfirming Questions:

Reframe your thinking by asking, "What would prove me wrong?" or "What evidence would change my mind?"

Example: If you think you should buy a house, ask, "What factors might make renting a better option?"

Everyday Example of Confirmation Bias

Imagine you're shopping for a phone. You've already decided on a brand, so you only read glowing reviews for that model while ignoring critical feedback about its battery life. To combat this, actively search for negative reviews to ensure you're making an informed choice.

Common Pitfalls When Addressing Confirmation Bias

1. Avoiding Discomfort:

It's natural to feel defensive when your beliefs are challenged, but growth happens when you confront uncomfortable truths.

2. Overvaluing Familiar Sources:

People often trust sources that align with their views, even if those sources are biased.

3. Cherry-Picking Data:

Selectively focusing on evidence that supports your beliefs reinforces the bias.

Takeaway

Confirmation Bias narrows your perspective and weakens your decision-making. By seeking out opposing evidence, asking challenging questions, and engaging with diverse viewpoints, you can expand your understanding and make better-informed choices.

Look Beyond the Brightest Star.

Most Memorable Example

Relevant Data

Chapter 23: Availability Heuristic

What Is the Availability Heuristic?

The Availability Heuristic is a mental shortcut where you rely on the most immediate examples that come to mind to make decisions. While quick and intuitive, this tendency can distort your judgment by overemphasizing memorable or recent events while ignoring broader data or less vivid possibilities.

Example:

After hearing about a plane crash on the news, you might think air travel is unsafe, even though statistically, it's one of the safest modes of transportation.

Why the Availability Heuristic Matters

1. Skews Risk Perception:

You're more likely to fear dramatic, rare events (like shark attacks) than more common, mundane risks (like car accidents) because the former are easier to recall.

2. Leads to Overgeneralization:

Decisions based on a single vivid example might not reflect the full picture.

3. Neglects Relevant Data:

By focusing on memorable stories or recent events, you may ignore broader, more reliable information.

How to Overcome the Availability Heuristic

1. Pause and Reflect:

When a vivid example influences your thinking, ask, "Am I basing this decision on a single event or broader evidence?"

Example: Before deciding not to invest in stocks after hearing about a market crash, reflect on long-term trends rather than short-term headlines.

2. Seek Statistical Data:

Look for objective data to balance emotional or anecdotal examples.

Example: If you're worried about crime in your neighborhood after hearing one story, review crime statistics to understand the actual risk.

3. Broaden Your Perspective:

Actively search for additional examples that challenge the one dominating your thoughts.

Example: If you're convinced starting a business is too risky because one friend failed, talk to others who succeeded to gain a balanced view.

4. Be Wary of Media Bias:

The news often highlights sensational stories, which can skew your perception of reality.

Example: Just because the media reports frequently on airline delays doesn't mean they happen often — it just means they're attention-grabbing.

Everyday Example of the Availability Heuristic

You hear about someone winning the lottery and think buying tickets is a good investment. However, the vivid example of their win overshadows the reality: the odds of winning are astronomically low. By reviewing the actual probability, you can avoid letting one story determine your choices.

Common Pitfalls When Addressing the Availability Heuristic

1. Focusing on Emotional Stories:

Emotional examples feel compelling but often don't represent the bigger picture.

2. Ignoring Silent Evidence:

The stories you don't hear — like all the startups that failed quietly — are just as important as the ones you do.

3. Overreacting to Recent Events:

Recent examples may feel more relevant but aren't always the most significant.

Takeaway

The Availability Heuristic tempts you to rely on what's easy to recall, but clear decisions require looking deeper. By broadening your perspective, seeking data, and challenging dramatic examples, you can make choices based on reality, not just what's memorable.

Chapter 24: Sunk Cost Fallacy

What Is the Sunk Cost Fallacy?

The Sunk Cost Fallacy is the tendency to stick with a decision because you've already invested time, money, or effort into it, even when continuing no longer makes sense. It's driven by a fear of "wasting" those resources, even though they're already gone and can't be recovered.

Example:

You stay in a bad relationship because you've been together for years, even though it no longer makes you happy.

Why the Sunk Cost Fallacy Matters

1. Wastes Resources:

Continuing to invest in a failing endeavor diverts time, money, and energy away from better opportunities.

2. Prevents Better Decisions:

Clinging to the past blinds you to present and future possibilities.

3. Reinforces Emotional Attachment:

The more you've invested, the harder it feels to let go, creating a vicious cycle.

Example in Action:

You've spent $10,000 repairing an old car, but it keeps breaking down. Instead of cutting your losses and buying a new car, you keep repairing it, sinking more money into a bad investment.

How to Break Free from the Sunk Cost Fallacy

1. Focus on the Present and Future:

Ask yourself: "If I hadn't already invested in this, would I still make the same decision today?"

Example: If you've spent months on a failing project, consider whether continuing aligns with your current goals.

2. Acknowledge the Loss:

Accept that the resources you've invested are gone and can't be recovered. This mental reset helps you focus on what's still within your control.

Example: Recognize that the time spent in a toxic friendship doesn't obligate you to maintain it.

3. Evaluate Opportunity Costs:

Think about what you're giving up by continuing down the same path.

Example: Sticking with a struggling business might prevent you from exploring a new, more promising venture.

4. Set Clear Criteria for Persistence:

Define specific benchmarks for continuing or stopping, so you're not swayed by emotion.

Example: "I'll invest one more month into this project. If we don't achieve X result, I'll move on."

Everyday Example of the Sunk Cost Fallacy

You're watching a boring movie but refuse to leave because you paid for the ticket. Letting go of the fallacy means recognizing that staying won't bring back your money — but leaving frees up your time for something more enjoyable.

Common Pitfalls When Addressing the Sunk Cost Fallacy

1. Fear of Admitting Failure:

People often equate quitting with failure, even when it's the smartest move.

2. Overvaluing Past Investments:

Emotional attachment to your efforts can cloud your judgment.

3. Ignoring Future Costs:

Focusing only on what's already lost blinds you to the additional resources you'll waste by continuing.

Takeaway

The Sunk Cost Fallacy tempts you to throw good money, time, or effort after bad. By focusing on the present and future instead of clinging to the past, you can free yourself to pursue better opportunities.

Chapter 25: Overconfidence Bias

What Is Overconfidence Bias?

Overconfidence Bias is the tendency to overestimate your knowledge, skills, or ability to predict outcomes. While confidence is valuable, overconfidence creates blind spots, leading you to underestimate risks, overlook critical details, or assume you're more prepared than you actually are.

Example:

You might believe you can finish a major project in half the time it actually takes, only to find yourself scrambling as deadlines approach.

Why Overconfidence Bias Matters

1. Increases Risk of Failure:

Overconfidence often leads to poor preparation, as you assume success is guaranteed.

2. Blinds You to Weaknesses:

When you overestimate your skills or knowledge, you're less likely to seek help or advice.

3. Leads to Overcommitment:

Overconfidence can make you take on too much, assuming you can handle it all effortlessly.

Example in Action:

A new investor might believe they can beat the stock market based on limited research. Overconfidence in their "gut instincts" could lead to losses they didn't anticipate.

How to Overcome Overconfidence Bias

1. Embrace Humility:

Acknowledge that you don't know everything. This mindset opens you up to learning and reduces the likelihood of making reckless decisions.

Example: Instead of assuming you'll ace a job interview, prepare thoroughly by practicing answers and researching the company.

2. Seek Objective Feedback:

Ask others to evaluate your plans or performance. A fresh perspective often reveals blind spots.

Example: Before launching a product, gather honest feedback from potential users rather than relying solely on your assumptions.

3. Double-Check Your Assumptions:

Challenge your beliefs by asking, "What evidence do I have that I'm right?"

Example: If you assume you can finish a task in a day, break it into steps and estimate the time for each. This forces you to confront the actual workload.

4. Plan for Contingencies:

Assume that things might not go as planned. Create backup strategies to manage risks.

Example: If you're starting a business, consider what you'll do if your initial idea doesn't gain traction.

Everyday Example of Overconfidence Bias

You believe you can drive to the airport in 30 minutes, so you leave just in time. However, you didn't account for traffic, construction, or finding parking, causing you to miss your flight. A more realistic approach would have included extra time for unforeseen delays.

Common Pitfalls in Overconfidence Bias

1. Ignoring Warning Signs:

Overconfidence often blinds you to red flags, such as missed deadlines or mounting risks.

2. Underestimating Complexity:

Overconfident decisions often fail to account for all the moving parts of a problem.

3. Resisting Help:

Overconfidence can make you reluctant to delegate or seek expert advice, leading to preventable mistakes.

Takeaway

Overconfidence Bias creates blind spots that can derail even the most promising plans. By embracing humility, seeking feedback, and preparing for risks, you can make more grounded, realistic decisions that lead to better outcomes.

Chapter 26: Framing Effect

What Is the Framing Effect?

The Framing Effect is the tendency for your decisions to be influenced by how information is presented, rather than the information itself. The same fact, framed differently, can lead to completely different reactions.

Example:

If a surgery has a "90% success rate," you'll likely feel optimistic. But if the same surgery is described as having a "10% failure rate," it feels much riskier — even though the facts are identical.

Why the Framing Effect Matters

1. Skews Your Judgment:

Framing can push you toward irrational decisions by emphasizing either the positives or negatives of a situation.

2. Limits Objectivity:

Decisions made under the influence of framing often ignore the full context.

3. Influences Marketing and Persuasion:

Advertisers and negotiators often use framing to sway your choices, making you feel like you're getting a better deal than you are.

Example in Action:

You're deciding between two sales offers:

- "Save $200!"

- "Spend $800!"

Although the deals are identical, the "Save $200" framing feels more appealing.

How to Overcome the Framing Effect

1. Rephrase the Problem:

Look at the situation from multiple angles. Ask, "How would I feel if this were framed differently?"

Example: When choosing between "80% lean" beef and "20% fat" beef, remember they're the same product.

2. Focus on the Data:

Strip away emotional language and focus on the raw numbers or facts.

Example: Instead of reacting to a "limited-time 50% off" sale, calculate the actual cost and compare it to your budget.

3. Consider the Opposite Frame:

Intentionally flip the framing to see if it changes your perception.

Example: If someone emphasizes the low risk of an investment, reframe it by focusing on the potential losses to assess whether it's worth it.

4. Ask Neutral Questions:

Avoid leading questions that emphasize one frame over another.

Example: Instead of asking, "How great is this deal?" ask, "How does this deal compare to others?"

Everyday Example of the Framing Effect

Imagine you're at a restaurant, and the menu highlights "Chef's Special — Only $19.99!" While it sounds like a bargain, reframing it as "$20 for one meal" might make you reconsider whether it's truly worth the price.

Common Pitfalls in Addressing the Framing Effect

1. Trusting Emotional Language:

Phrases like "only," "save," or "best deal" are designed to appeal emotionally but often lack context.

2. Ignoring Alternative Perspectives:

Failing to explore other frames keeps you locked into a narrow view.

3. Assuming You're Immune:

The Framing Effect is subtle and influences everyone, even if you think you're too rational to be swayed.

Takeaway

The Framing Effect shows how much presentation matters in decision-making. By reframing problems, focusing on the raw facts, and questioning emotional language, you can make clearer, more rational choices.

Chapter 27: Loss Aversion

What Is Loss Aversion?

Loss Aversion is the tendency to fear losses more intensely than you value equivalent gains. For most people, losing $100 feels far worse than the satisfaction of gaining $100. This fear of loss can lead you to avoid risks, even when the potential rewards outweigh the downside.

Example:

You're hesitant to invest in a promising business because you're more worried about losing your initial capital than excited about the potential returns.

Why Loss Aversion Matters

1. Leads to Missed Opportunities:

Fear of loss often keeps you from pursuing high-reward ventures, such as investing, starting a new project, or making a career change.

2. Encourages Risky Behavior to Avoid Losses:

Ironically, loss aversion can also make you double down on bad decisions just to avoid admitting failure.

3. Distorts Decision-Making:

By focusing too much on avoiding losses, you fail to evaluate decisions logically or holistically.

Example in Action:

A homeowner might refuse to sell their property at a slight loss, even if reinvesting the money elsewhere could yield greater financial returns.

How to Overcome Loss Aversion

1. Reframe Losses as Learning:

Instead of seeing every loss as a failure, view it as an opportunity to grow.

Example: If a business idea doesn't succeed, focus on the skills, experience, and lessons you gained rather than the lost investment.

2. Shift Focus to Potential Gains:

When evaluating risks, actively think about the rewards to balance your perspective.

Example: If you're considering a career switch, imagine the new skills, opportunities, and satisfaction you'll gain rather than fearing temporary uncertainty.

3. Use Data to Ground Decisions:

Base your choices on probabilities and outcomes, not on emotional reactions to potential losses.

Example: If the odds of succeeding in an investment are high and the risk is calculated, let the numbers guide you, not your fear.

4. Set Limits on Emotional Influence:

Establish clear decision criteria to prevent fear from taking over.

Example: If you're nervous about selling an underperforming stock, decide in advance to sell if it drops below a certain threshold, avoiding emotional hesitation.

Everyday Example of Loss Aversion

You're offered a refund guarantee when buying a product but hesitate because returning it feels like "admitting defeat." By reframing the return as a smart financial move rather than a loss, you make a better decision.

Common Pitfalls in Overcoming Loss Aversion

1. Overcompensating:

In an attempt to overcome loss aversion, some people take reckless risks without proper evaluation.

2. Dwelling on Past Losses:

Focusing on previous setbacks can amplify your fear of future risks.

3. Neglecting Long-Term Gains:

Loss aversion often prioritizes short-term comfort over long-term rewards.

Takeaway

Loss Aversion is a powerful emotional bias, but it doesn't have to control you. By reframing losses, focusing on gains, and grounding your decisions in logic, you can embrace opportunities that fear might otherwise block.

Chapter 28: Hindsight Bias

What Is Hindsight Bias?

Hindsight Bias is the tendency to see past events as more predictable than they actually were. Once an outcome is known, it's easy to say, "I knew that would happen!" — even if you didn't. This illusion of foresight can lead to unfair self-criticism or overconfidence in future decisions.

Example:

After a stock market crash, you might think, "I should have seen that coming," forgetting that the market's behavior was uncertain at the time.

Why Hindsight Bias Matters

1. Leads to Unfair Self-Judgment:

Believing you "should have known better" creates unnecessary guilt or regret.

2. Skews Future Decisions:

Overconfidence in your predictive ability can make you underestimate risks.

3. Hinders Learning:

If you think the outcome was obvious, you're less likely to analyze what actually influenced the result.

How to Overcome Hindsight Bias

1. Acknowledge Uncertainty:

Remind yourself that past events seemed unclear at the time, even if they feel predictable now.

Example: Instead of thinking, "I should have avoided that failed investment," acknowledge the market data didn't guarantee success or failure.

2. Analyze Context, Not Outcomes:

Focus on the factors that influenced your decision, rather than judging based solely on the result.

Example: If you chose a job that didn't work out, consider whether you made the best choice based on the information you had then.

3. Document Decisions:

Write down your reasoning at the time of a decision. Reviewing it later helps you see what you knew — and didn't know — at the moment.

4. Seek Feedback:

Share your decision-making process with others to gain perspective and avoid bias.

Example: A mentor can help you see whether your choices were reasonable, regardless of the outcome.

Everyday Example of Hindsight Bias

You're planning a picnic, and it rains. Looking back, you think, "I should've checked the weather." But if the forecast showed only a slight chance of rain, the decision was reasonable. Recognizing this prevents unnecessary self-blame.

Common Pitfalls in Addressing Hindsight Bias

1. Overconfidence in Predictions:

Thinking you "knew it all along" can lead to poor preparation in the future.

2. Ignoring External Factors:

Outcomes often depend on factors beyond your control.

3. Fixating on Results:

Focusing only on whether a decision succeeded or failed oversimplifies its complexity.

Takeaway

Hindsight Bias can make the past seem deceptively clear, leading to unfair self-judgment and overconfidence. By focusing on the decision-making process rather than outcomes, you can learn from the past without distorting it.

Chapter 29: Groupthink

What Is Groupthink?

Groupthink occurs when a group prioritizes harmony and consensus over critical thinking. This bias pushes people to conform to the majority's view, even if they disagree internally or spot potential flaws. The result? Poor decisions that could have been avoided with independent perspectives.

Example:

A team approves a risky business strategy without raising objections because no one wants to disrupt the meeting's positive mood or challenge the boss's opinion.

Why Groupthink Matters

1. Suppresses Dissenting Voices:

In a desire to "keep the peace," individuals may avoid sharing valuable insights or concerns.

2. Leads to Suboptimal Decisions:

By focusing on agreement, groups often ignore critical risks, alternative solutions, or weaknesses in their plans.

3. Promotes Overconfidence in the Group:

A false sense of certainty arises because everyone appears to agree, even if that agreement is shallow or coerced.

Historical Example:

The Bay of Pigs invasion in 1961 is a classic example of Groupthink. U.S. officials failed to question the plan's feasibility, leading to a widely criticized failure.

How to Overcome Groupthink

1. Encourage Diverse Opinions:

Leaders should actively invite dissent and create a safe space for different perspectives.

Example: A team leader could say, "Let's discuss why this idea might not work and what other options we should consider."

2. Appoint a Devil's Advocate:

Designate someone to deliberately challenge the group's assumptions.

Example: In brainstorming sessions, one team member could question the feasibility of each proposed solution.

3. Emphasize Evidence Over Consensus:

Shift the focus from agreement to data and logic.

Example: Instead of voting on the best strategy, ask, "What do the numbers suggest?" or "What's the evidence supporting this decision?"

4. Encourage Anonymous Feedback:

Allow group members to share concerns or suggestions privately to reduce the fear of judgment.

Example: Use anonymous surveys or suggestion boxes during major planning sessions.

5. Break the Group into Smaller Teams:

Smaller groups are less likely to succumb to Groupthink and can independently explore alternative solutions.

Everyday Example of Groupthink

You're dining with friends, and everyone agrees to eat at a certain restaurant. You dislike the choice but stay quiet to avoid conflict. Overcoming Groupthink means speaking up — "Hey, I'd prefer a different spot. Can we consider other options?" — and opening the floor for discussion.

Common Pitfalls in Addressing Groupthink

1. Fear of Rejection:

Many people hesitate to challenge the group, worrying it might create tension or make them seem difficult.

2. Assuming Silence Equals Agreement:

Just because no one objects doesn't mean everyone agrees.

3. Overvaluing Consensus:

Group leaders often mistake unity for progress, ignoring whether the solution is actually sound.

Takeaway

Groupthink prioritizes harmony at the expense of sound decisions. By fostering diverse perspectives, encouraging dissent, and emphasizing evidence over agreement, you can make stronger, more balanced choices.

I just read one article about coding. I could probably build the company website this weekend!
You might want to learn about backend systems and security first.

Chapter 30: The Dunning-Kruger Effect

What Is the Dunning-Kruger Effect?

The Dunning-Kruger Effect describes the tendency for people with limited knowledge or skills in a specific area to overestimate their competence. Ironically, those who know the least are often the most confident, while experts, who recognize the complexities, are more humble about their knowledge.

Example:

A novice cook might believe they can run a successful restaurant after preparing a few impressive meals, ignoring the complexities of staffing, budgeting, and menu planning.

Why the Dunning-Kruger Effect Matters

1. Leads to Poor Decisions:

Overconfidence in your abilities may lead you to take on challenges you're unprepared for.

2. Discourages Learning:

Believing you already "know enough" prevents you from seeking new knowledge or skills.

3. Creates Miscommunication:

Those affected by the Dunning-Kruger Effect may reject expert advice, assuming they know better.

How to Overcome the Dunning-Kruger Effect

1. Embrace Lifelong Learning:

Recognize that expertise requires continuous effort and learning.

Example: Instead of assuming you're an expert after reading one article, commit to studying the subject more deeply.

2. Seek Feedback from Experts:

Ask experienced individuals to evaluate your knowledge or skills.

Example: If you're starting a business, consult with seasoned entrepreneurs to identify gaps in your plan.

3. Practice Intellectual Humility:

Acknowledge what you don't know and be willing to learn.

Example: Instead of saying, "I know how to manage a team," say, "I'm still learning what makes a great leader. Can you share advice?"

4. Ask Better Questions:

Shift from assuming you have the answers to seeking deeper understanding.

Example: If you're tackling a technical challenge, ask, "What am I missing here?" instead of assuming you've covered all bases.

5. Review Past Mistakes:

Reflect on instances where overconfidence led to poor outcomes and identify what you could have done differently.

Example: If a DIY project went wrong, analyze what steps you skipped or underestimated.

Everyday Example of the Dunning-Kruger Effect

You take a few fitness classes and start advising others on exercise routines, only to realize later that your advice overlooked critical factors like injury prevention and nutrition. Recognizing this, you decide to study more before offering advice.

Common Pitfalls in Addressing the Dunning-Kruger Effect

1. Resisting Feedback:

Overconfident individuals often dismiss constructive criticism, assuming they know better.

2. Mistaking Initial Success for Mastery:

Early wins can create a false sense of expertise.

3. Overgeneralizing Knowledge:

Being skilled in one area doesn't automatically translate to expertise in others.

Takeaway

The Dunning-Kruger Effect teaches that true expertise begins with recognizing what you don't know. By seeking feedback, embracing humility, and committing to learning, you can build genuine competence and make more informed decisions.

Part IV: Tools and Techniques for Rational Decision-Making

In this section, I introduce you to powerful tools and structured techniques for making clear, well-informed decisions. Whether you're solving complex problems or navigating uncertainty, these methods help break down options and improve outcomes.

"If we spend three hours studying math, we might ace the test, but if we divide the time between subjects, our overall grades could improve.

Let's add what happens if we focus on just one weak subject first!

Chapter 31: The Decision Tree

What is a Decision Tree?

A Decision Tree is a tool to visually map choices, their potential outcomes, and subsequent decisions. It helps you understand how one choice leads to another, allowing you to evaluate the long-term consequences and risks of each path.

Why Decision Trees Matter

Decision-making often involves uncertainty, complexity, or hidden trade-offs. A Decision Tree simplifies this by laying out all possible paths, making it easier to compare them objectively. It's especially useful when choices involve multiple steps or outcomes.

Example: Choosing a Marketing Strategy

Imagine you need to decide between two marketing campaigns:

- **Option 1:** Invest in social media ads.

    o **Outcome 1:** Increased traffic but higher costs.

    o **Outcome 2:** Minimal traffic and wasted investment.

- • **Option 2:** Launch email marketing.

    o **Outcome 1:** Moderate traffic but high engagement.

    o **Outcome 2:** No improvement in sales.

Mapping this as a tree clarifies which option offers the best chance of meeting your goals.

How to Create a Decision Tree

1. **Start with a Decision:** Define the question or choice you're facing.

2. **List Options:** Identify all possible actions you can take.

3. **Add Outcomes:** For each option, map potential results, including secondary decisions.

4. **Estimate Probabilities:** Assign likelihoods to each outcome to evaluate risk.

5. **Weigh Results:** Use costs, benefits, or probabilities to determine the best path.

Everyday Example

You're deciding between walking, biking, or driving to work.

- **Option 1:** Walk.

    o **Outcome 1:** Arrive refreshed but take longer.

    o **Outcome 2:** Risk being late if the weather changes.

- **Option 2:** Bike.

    o **Outcome 1:** Save time but risk an accident.

- **Option 3:** Drive.

    o **Outcome 1:** Arrive quickly but incur parking costs.

The tree visually highlights trade-offs between time, cost, and convenience.

Common Pitfalls in Decision Trees

1. **Overcomplicating Branches:** Too many details can overwhelm the analysis.

2. **Inaccurate Probabilities:** Make sure estimates are realistic.

3. **Ignoring Intangibles:** Factors like personal values or intuition may not fit neatly into a tree but still matter.

Takeaway

A Decision Tree organizes your choices and clarifies trade-offs, making complex decisions easier to approach logically. It's a simple yet powerful way to evaluate paths and their outcomes.

EMOTIONS

CAUTION

FACTS

OPTIMISM

CREATIVITY

CONTROL

Chapter 32: The Six Thinking Hats

What are the Six Thinking Hats?

The Six Thinking Hats is a structured thinking tool developed by Edward de Bono. Each hat represents a different mode of thinking, encouraging you to approach problems from multiple perspectives to ensure a balanced and thorough evaluation.

Why the Six Thinking Hats Matter

Most people default to one way of thinking—logical, emotional, or cautious. This tool forces you to examine problems from all angles, fostering creativity, identifying risks, and uncovering opportunities that might otherwise be overlooked.

1. **White Hat (Facts):** Focus on data, evidence, and objective information.

2. **Red Hat (Emotions):** Consider gut feelings, instincts, and emotional reactions.

3. **Black Hat (Caution):** Identify potential risks, weaknesses, or obstacles.

4. **Yellow Hat (Optimism):** Highlight the benefits and positive aspects of a solution.

5. **Green Hat (Creativity):** Brainstorm innovative ideas and alternative approaches.

6. **Blue Hat (Control):** Manage the thinking process and ensure all hats are used appropriately.

Example: Planning a New Business Venture

Imagine starting a bakery:

- **White Hat:** What is the market size? What are typical startup costs?

- **Red Hat:** How passionate do you feel about running a bakery?

- **Black Hat:** What if demand is lower than expected? What are your risks?

- **Yellow Hat:** What opportunities exist in your local area?

- **Green Hat:** Could you offer unique products, like gluten-free pastries?

- **Blue Hat:** Have you considered all perspectives fairly?

Using these hats ensures no critical aspect of the venture is overlooked.

How to Use the Six Thinking Hats

1. **Start with One Hat:** Focus on one perspective at a time to avoid bias.

2. **Switch Hats:** Rotate through each hat systematically to cover all angles.

3. **Combine Insights:** Synthesize findings from all hats to create a well-rounded solution.

Common Pitfalls in Using the Hats

1. **Skipping Perspectives:** Avoid ignoring hats you find uncomfortable or irrelevant.

2. **Overanalyzing:** Don't spend too much time on one hat, especially if it dominates the process.

3. **Ignoring Intuition:** While structured, the Red Hat allows emotions to play a role in decision-making.

Takeaway

The Six Thinking Hats fosters balanced, creative, and cautious thinking by examining a problem from all perspectives. It's a versatile tool for better decisions and innovative solutions.

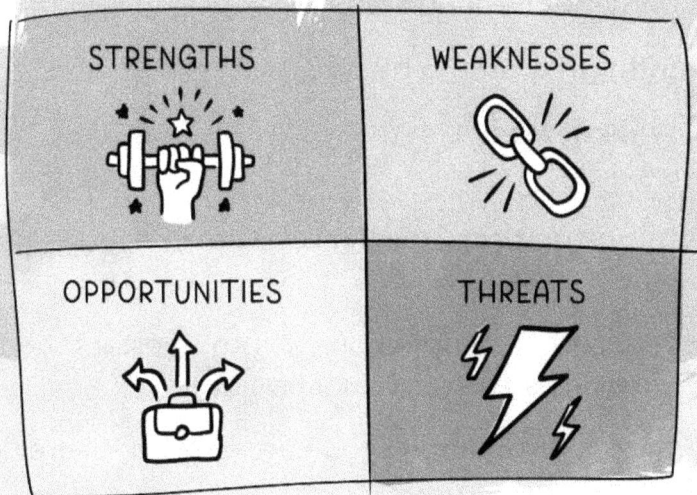

Chapter 33: SWOT Analysis

What is SWOT Analysis?

SWOT Analysis is a strategic framework used to evaluate internal and external factors affecting a decision, goal, or project. The four quadrants—Strengths, Weaknesses, Opportunities, and Threats—offer a structured way to identify advantages, risks, and areas for improvement.

Why SWOT Analysis Matters

SWOT helps you assess the current situation holistically by balancing internal capabilities (strengths and weaknesses) with external realities (opportunities and threats). It's particularly effective for strategic planning and risk assessment.

Example: Expanding a Business

Imagine you're considering opening a second location:

- **Strengths:** Strong brand loyalty, experienced staff.

- **Weaknesses:** Limited cash flow, lack of marketing expertise.

- **Opportunities:** Growing demand in a neighboring city, reduced lease costs.

- **Threats:** Competition from established local businesses, economic uncertainty.

By analyzing these factors, you can make a clearer decision about whether and how to proceed.

How to Conduct a SWOT Analysis

1. **Identify Strengths:** What internal resources or advantages set you apart?

2. **Spot Weaknesses:** Where are your vulnerabilities or limitations?

3. **Explore Opportunities:** What external trends, gaps, or partnerships could you leverage?

4. **Acknowledge Threats:** What external risks or obstacles could harm you?

Everyday Example of SWOT Analysis

Suppose you're deciding whether to pursue a new career opportunity:

- **Strengths:** Relevant skills, strong professional network.

- **Weaknesses:** Limited industry experience.

- **Opportunities:** Potential for career growth and higher income.

- **Threats:** Uncertainty about the company's future.

SWOT helps you make an informed decision by clarifying pros and cons.

Common Pitfalls in SWOT Analysis

1. **Ignoring Weaknesses:** Be honest about limitations; sugar-coating weak points undermines the process.

2. **Overestimating Opportunities:** Avoid being overly optimistic without data to back it up.

3. **Inaction:** Insights from SWOT are only valuable if followed by concrete actions.

Takeaway

SWOT Analysis offers a structured way to evaluate decisions by balancing internal and external factors. Use it to identify strengths, mitigate risks, and seize opportunities with confidence.

Criteria	Weight	Requirement score				
		A	B	C	D	E
Value	20%	80	45	40	15	35
Risk	20%	60	85	30	20	75
Difficulty	15%	55	80	50	15	25
Success	10%	30	60	55	65	30
Compliance	5%	35	50	60	50	50
Relationships	5%	80	70	50	85	80
Stakeholder	15%	25	50	45	60	60
Urgency	10%	60	25	40	65	80
Weighted Scores	100%	54.8	60.0	43.3	38.0	52.3

Chapter 34: Weighted Scoring

What is Weighted Scoring?

Weighted Scoring is a method to rank options based on criteria that matter most to you. By assigning weights (importance) and scores (performance) to each criterion, you calculate a total score for every option, making complex decisions easier and more objective.

Why Weighted Scoring Matters

Decisions often involve multiple factors, and not all are equally important. Weighted Scoring allows you to prioritize what matters most and compare options systematically, reducing guesswork and bias.

Example: Choosing a New Apartment

Suppose you're choosing between three apartments. Your criteria are Cost, Location, and Size.

- Assign **weights** to each criterion (e.g., Cost = 50%, Location = 30%, Size = 20%).

- Score each apartment based on how well it performs in each category (e.g., Cost: 8/10).

- Multiply the weight by the score to calculate a weighted score for each option.

The apartment with the highest total score becomes your best choice.

How to Use Weighted Scoring

1. **List Criteria:** Identify the factors that influence your decision.

2. **Assign Weights:** Allocate importance to each criterion, ensuring they add up to 100%.

3. **Score Options:** Evaluate how well each option performs against the criteria.

4. **Calculate Totals:** Multiply each score by its weight, then sum the totals for each option.

5. **Rank Results:** Use the total scores to rank your choices.

Everyday Example of Weighted Scoring

Imagine deciding which smartphone to buy based on Price, Features, and Battery Life.

- Price = 40% weight, Features = 40% weight, Battery Life = 20% weight.

- Option 1 scores 9/10 in Price, 7/10 in Features, and 8/10 in Battery Life.

- Weighted Score = (9×0.4) + (7×0.4) + (8×0.2) = 8.2.

Compare scores across all options to identify the best fit.

Common Pitfalls in Weighted Scoring

1. **Overcomplicating Criteria:** Too many factors dilute focus. Stick to 3–5 key criteria.

2. **Unbalanced Weights:** Ensure weights reflect true priorities. Overemphasis on minor factors skews results.

3. **Subjective Scoring:** Be consistent and objective when assigning scores.

Takeaway

Weighted Scoring helps you prioritize what matters and make objective decisions by balancing multiple factors. It's a simple, reliable way to compare complex options and identify the best fit.

Chapter 35: Scenario Planning

What is Scenario Planning?

Scenario Planning is a tool to prepare for uncertainty by imagining different possible futures. By envisioning "best-case," "worst-case," and "most likely" scenarios, you can develop strategies to handle whatever comes your way.

Why Scenario Planning Matters

The future is unpredictable, and decisions based on a single assumption can fail when conditions change. Scenario Planning builds flexibility, helping you anticipate risks, adapt to challenges, and seize opportunities in a variety of situations.

Example: Expanding a Business

Suppose you're planning to expand into a new market.

- **Best Case:** Strong demand leads to rapid growth.
- **Worst Case:** Demand is weak, and the investment fails.
- **Most Likely Case:** Moderate growth with manageable challenges.

By preparing strategies for each scenario—like setting aside extra funds for risks—you ensure success under different circumstances.

How to Practice Scenario Planning

1. **Define Key Factors:** Identify the uncertainties most likely to impact your decision (e.g., economic trends, competition).

2. **Create Scenarios:** Develop at least three scenarios: best-case, worst-case, and most likely outcomes.

3. **Analyze Impacts:** Assess how each scenario would affect your goals or plans.

4. **Plan Responses:** Develop strategies to maximize benefits or minimize risks for each scenario.

5. **Monitor Trends**: Adjust your plans as new information becomes available.

Everyday Example of Scenario Planning

Imagine saving for a vacation but unsure about your future expenses.

- **Best Case:** You receive a bonus and can afford luxury travel.

- **Worst Case:** An unexpected expense forces you to delay plans.

- **Most Likely Case:** You stick to a modest budget.

By planning for all three, you avoid surprises and enjoy peace of mind.

Common Pitfalls in Scenario Planning

1. **Too Many Scenarios:** Stick to a manageable number (3–5) to avoid confusion.

2. **Neglecting Extreme Cases:** Don't ignore low-probability but high-impact risks.

3. **Failing to Monitor Trends:** Scenario plans are only useful if updated as conditions change.

Takeaway

Scenario Planning helps you navigate uncertainty by preparing for multiple outcomes. With flexible strategies, you're ready for anything.

Chapter 36: Pre-Mortem Analysis

What is a Pre-Mortem Analysis?

A Pre-Mortem Analysis involves imagining that a decision or project has already failed, then identifying the reasons why. By working backward, you uncover risks and weak points before they occur, allowing you to address them proactively.

Why Pre-Mortem Analysis Matters

Optimism bias can blind us to potential failures, causing avoidable mistakes. A Pre-Mortem forces you to confront risks early, improving your chances of success by anticipating and addressing problems in advance.

Example: Planning a Product Launch

Suppose you're launching a new app. In your Pre-Mortem, you ask, "What could cause this launch to fail?"

- **Answer 1:** Marketing didn't reach the right audience.

- **Answer 2:** The app had bugs at release.

- **Answer 3:** Competitors launched a similar product first.

By identifying these risks, you adjust your plan to avoid failure.

How to Conduct a Pre-Mortem Analysis

1. **Imagine Failure:** Assume your decision has failed catastrophically.

2. **Ask Why:** Brainstorm reasons for the failure, focusing on overlooked risks or weak points.

3. **List Fixes:** Identify ways to address or prevent each potential problem.

4. **Adjust the Plan:** Integrate these fixes into your strategy before moving forward.

Everyday Example of a Pre-Mortem

You're planning a wedding. A Pre-Mortem might reveal risks like weather issues, late vendors, or seating conflicts. By addressing these risks—reserving a tent, confirming vendors early, and creating a seating plan—you reduce the likelihood of chaos.

Common Pitfalls in Pre-Mortem Analysis

1. **Overemphasizing Negatives:** Focus on realistic risks, not exaggerated fears.

2. **Ignoring Fixes:** Identifying risks is useless unless you take action to address them.

3. **Skipping Collaboration:** Involve others to uncover blind spots.

Takeaway

A Pre-Mortem Analysis transforms potential failure into a learning opportunity, helping you refine your decisions before committing. By planning for setbacks, you strengthen your strategy and improve your chances of success.

Chapter 37: Monte Carlo Simulation

What is Monte Carlo Simulation?

Monte Carlo Simulation is a method to model uncertainty by running multiple simulations of a decision or event. By using random variables to represent uncertainty, it provides a range of possible outcomes and their probabilities, helping you make informed predictions.

Why Monte Carlo Simulation Matters

In complex decisions, there's rarely one "guaranteed" outcome. Monte Carlo Simulation helps you account for variability and uncertainty, showing not just what could happen but how likely it is to happen. It's particularly valuable in finance, project planning, and risk management.

Example: Estimating a Project Budget

Imagine budgeting for a construction project. You're unsure about the costs of labor, materials, and potential delays.

- Run simulations using ranges for each variable (e.g., labor costs might vary between $50k and $70k).

- The simulation generates thousands of potential budgets, showing that 70% of outcomes fall between $120k and $140k.

This insight allows you to plan for uncertainty and avoid underfunding.

How to Use Monte Carlo Simulation

1. **Define Variables:** Identify key factors that influence your decision (e.g., costs, demand, timelines).

2. **Assign Ranges:** Use realistic ranges for each variable instead of fixed numbers.

3. **Simulate Outcomes:** Run multiple simulations, varying the inputs randomly within their ranges.

4. **Analyze Results:** Examine the distribution of outcomes to identify patterns and probabilities.

5. **Plan Accordingly:** Use insights to prepare for the most likely scenarios and mitigate risks.

Everyday Example of Monte Carlo Simulation

Suppose you're planning a vacation but uncertain about costs. Estimate ranges for flights, accommodations, and activities, then run a simulation to predict total expenses. If 80% of outcomes fit your budget, you can move forward confidently.

Common Pitfalls in Monte Carlo Simulation

1. **Poor Assumptions:** Garbage in, garbage out—if your input ranges are unrealistic, your results will be too.

2. **Ignoring Outliers:** Rare but extreme outcomes may require special attention.

3. **Overcomplication:** Avoid adding unnecessary variables; focus on the most impactful ones.

Takeaway

Monte Carlo Simulation models uncertainty by showing the range and likelihood of possible outcomes. It's a powerful way to plan confidently in unpredictable situations.

CRITERIA	WEIGHT	SUPPLIER A	SUPPLIER B	SUPPLIER C
COST	40% (0.4)	8 (3,2)	7 (2,8)	9 (3,6)
QUALITY	35% (0,35)	9 (3,15)	8 (2,8)	7 (2,45)
DELIVERY SPEED	25% (0,25)	7 (1,75)	9 (2,25)	6 (1,5)
TOTAL SCORE		8,1	7,85	7,55

Chapter 38: Decision Matrices: Simplify Complex Choices

What is a Decision Matrix?

A Decision Matrix is a tool to compare multiple options against key criteria in a structured way. By assigning scores to each criterion, you calculate a total score for each option, helping you identify the best choice quickly and objectively.

Why Decision Matrix Matters

Complex decisions often involve multiple factors, and it's easy to overlook important details or let bias influence your choice. A Decision Matrix organizes information clearly, making comparisons straightforward and reducing emotional interference.

Example: Choosing a Supplier

Suppose you're deciding between three suppliers for your business. Your criteria are Cost, Quality, and Delivery Speed.

- Assign scores for each supplier based on performance in these areas.

- Total the scores to identify the best overall option. For instance:

    o Supplier A = Cost (8) + Quality (9) + Speed (7) = 24.

    o Supplier B = Cost (7) + Quality (8) + Speed (9) = 24.

    o Supplier C = Cost (9) + Quality (7) + Speed (6) = 22.

Supplier A and B tie, so you might consider extra factors to break the tie.

How to Use a Decision Matrix

1. **List Options and Criteria:** Identify what you're choosing between and the factors that matter.

2. **Weight Criteria (Optional):** Assign importance to each criterion if some matter more than others.

3. **Score Each Option:** Rate each option on a consistent scale (e.g., 1–10) for every criterion.

4. **Calculate Totals:** Sum the scores for each option to determine the winner.

Everyday Example of a Decision Matrix

Imagine deciding where to eat dinner with friends:

- **Criteria:** Price, Distance, Menu Variety.

- **Options:** Restaurant A, B, and C.

- **Scores:** Restaurant A (8, 9, 7) totals 24, making it the top choice.

The matrix makes the decision quick, fair, and transparent.

Common Pitfalls in Decision Matrix

1. **Overloading Criteria:** Focus on the most critical factors to avoid analysis paralysis.

2. **Subjective Scoring:** Be consistent and objective when assigning scores.

3. **Ignoring Weights:** If some criteria are more important, weight them to reflect their value.

Takeaway

A Decision Matrix simplifies choices by organizing options and criteria in a clear, comparable format. It's a reliable way to balance multiple factors and identify the best solution.

Factor	Pro/Con	Weight	Impact	Score
Better job opportunities	Pro	9	+8	+72
Exciting lifestyle	Pro	8	+7	+56
Higher cost of living	Con	7	−6	−42
Far from family	Con	6	−5	−30
Pros Total: +128	Cons Total: −72		Net Score: +56	

Chapter 39: Pro/Con Lists Done Right

What is a Pro/Con List?

A Pro/Con List is a simple tool to weigh the advantages and disadvantages of a decision. When done right, it goes beyond listing pros and cons by adding context, such as importance or likelihood, to make the decision clearer.

Why Pro/Con Lists Matter

Pro/Con Lists are quick and intuitive, but they're often too basic to guide major decisions. Adding context — such as weights or probabilities — turns them into powerful decision-making tools.

Example: Deciding Whether to Move to a New City

- **Pros:** Better job opportunities (+8), exciting lifestyle (+7).
- **Cons:** Higher cost of living (-6), far from family (-5).
- **Adjusted Score:** Add weights or importance to each factor to clarify whether the pros outweigh the cons.

How to Create a Pro/Con List Done Right

1. **List Pros and Cons:** Identify advantages and disadvantages of your decision.
2. **Assign Weights:** Rate how important each factor is (e.g., 1–10).
3. **Score Impact:** Assess the positive or negative impact of each factor.
4. **Calculate Totals:** Multiply weights by scores to determine the overall balance.

Everyday Example of a Pro/Con List

Imagine debating whether to adopt a pet:

- **Pros:** Companionship (+8), Increased happiness (+10).
- **Cons:** Costs (-6), Responsibility (-7).
- **Weighted Total:** The pros total +18, while the cons total -13, suggesting adoption is the better choice.

Common Pitfalls in Pro/Con Lists

1. **Vague Factors:** Be specific to avoid superficial results.
2. **Ignoring Context:** Without weights or impact, minor factors can skew results.
3. **Over-reliance:** Pro/Con Lists are one tool; combine them with others for big decisions.

Takeaway

Pro/Con Lists go beyond simple lists to incorporate context, making them a powerful yet intuitive decision-making tool.

Chapter 40: Heuristic Shortcuts

What Are Heuristic Shortcuts?

Heuristic shortcuts are mental strategies or "rules of thumb" that simplify decision-making. Instead of analyzing every detail, you rely on general guidelines to make quick, efficient choices. Heuristics are invaluable in fast-paced situations, but they're not without risks — their simplicity can sometimes lead to errors.

Example:

When deciding which book to buy, you might rely on a heuristic like "bestsellers are good" instead of reading every review. While efficient, this shortcut may overlook books that fit your taste but aren't on the bestseller list.

Why Heuristic Shortcuts Matter

1. Save Time and Energy:

Heuristics streamline decision-making, helping you avoid "analysis paralysis."

2. Enable Rapid Decisions:

In high-pressure situations, they let you act quickly without overthinking.

3. Provide Reliable Results (Most of the Time):

When applied appropriately, heuristics often yield satisfactory outcomes.

Example in Action:

You're grocery shopping and decide to buy the brand you've used before. This heuristic, "stick with what works," saves time compared to analyzing every option on the shelf.

How to Use Heuristic Shortcuts Wisely

1. Match the Shortcut to the Situation:

Heuristics work best in routine or low-stakes decisions. For complex or high-stakes choices, a more detailed analysis is better.

Example: Choosing where to eat dinner? A heuristic like "go to the highest-rated place nearby" works. Deciding on a career move? Take your time.

2. Combine with Logic:

Use heuristics as a starting point, but verify their relevance with critical thinking.

Example: If you use the heuristic "expensive items are higher quality," double-check reviews to confirm the product is worth the price.

3. Learn from Experience:

Over time, refine your shortcuts based on what works for you.

Example: If "choosing the middle option" often leads to good results, you can use it confidently in similar situations.

4. Be Aware of Cognitive Biases:

Some heuristics, like relying on recent memories (Availability Heuristic), can mislead you. Stay vigilant about potential errors.

Everyday Example of Heuristic Shortcuts

Imagine you're packing for a trip. Instead of creating a detailed checklist, you rely on the heuristic "pack what I used on my last trip." While efficient, this shortcut could miss new items you'll need for a different climate.

Common Pitfalls in Using Heuristics

1. Over-Reliance on Shortcuts:

Simplified rules can miss critical details in complex decisions.

2. Misapplying a Heuristic:

A rule that works in one context might fail in another.

3. Neglecting Better Options:

Heuristics focus on efficiency, not optimization, so you might miss opportunities for better results.

Takeaway

Heuristic shortcuts are powerful tools for saving time, but they're not a one-size-fits-all solution. By applying them thoughtfully and balancing them with critical thinking, you can make smarter, faster decisions without sacrificing accuracy.

Part V: Emotional Intelligence in Decision-Making

This section explores how mastering your emotions, understanding the feelings of others, and managing mental fatigue can transform the way you approach decisions. Remember: The best decisions aren't just smart — they're balanced, grounded, and deeply human.

Chapter 41: Self-Regulation

What Is Self-Regulation?

Self-regulation is the ability to manage your emotions, impulses, and reactions in a way that aligns with your goals. It's not about suppressing emotions but channeling them constructively, especially in high-pressure situations.

Example:

If someone criticizes you in a meeting, self-regulation means pausing to process your feelings instead of reacting defensively. This allows you to respond calmly and maintain professionalism.

Why Self-Regulation Matters in Decision-Making

1. Reduces Impulsive Choices:

Emotional reactions, like anger or excitement, can lead to rash decisions.

2. Improves Long-Term Outcomes:

By staying composed, you're more likely to make thoughtful choices that align with your goals.

3. Builds Trust and Credibility:

People who manage their emotions well are seen as reliable and level-headed.

Example in Action:

Imagine a business deal is delayed. Instead of panicking and making concessions, self-regulation helps you stay calm, negotiate effectively, and avoid unnecessary compromises.

How to Master Self-Regulation

1. Pause Before Reacting:

Take a deep breath or count to ten before responding in emotionally charged situations.

Example: If you receive a frustrating email, wait a few minutes before replying. This prevents a hasty, emotional response.

2. Label Your Emotions:

Naming what you feel (e.g., "I'm anxious" or "I'm frustrated") helps you process emotions instead of letting them control you.

Example: Acknowledging that you're nervous before a presentation can help you take proactive steps to calm yourself.

3. Focus on What You Can Control:

Redirect energy toward actions you can influence, rather than fixating on things beyond your control.

Example: Instead of stressing over a missed opportunity, focus on preparing for the next one.

4. Practice Emotional Awareness Daily:

Reflect on situations where emotions influenced your decisions. Ask yourself, "How could I have handled this better?"

Everyday Example of Self-Regulation

You're stuck in traffic and running late. Instead of letting frustration take over, you accept the situation, call ahead to explain, and use the time to listen to an audiobook. By regulating your emotions, you stay calm and productive.

Common Pitfalls in Self-Regulation

1. Suppressing Emotions:

Ignoring feelings doesn't resolve them — it often makes them resurface later in unproductive ways.

2. Overreacting to Small Triggers:

Small annoyances can escalate if you don't actively manage your reactions.

3. Neglecting Emotional Preparation:

Stressful situations are inevitable, but practicing self-regulation skills in advance can help you handle them more effectively.

Takeaway

Self-regulation is a cornerstone of emotional intelligence and decision-making. By learning to pause, process, and channel your emotions, you can make choices that reflect your best self rather than your immediate reactions.

Chapter 42: Empathy and Decisions

What Is Empathy in Decision-Making?

Empathy is the ability to understand and share the feelings of others. In decision-making, it means stepping into someone else's shoes to consider how your choices will impact them emotionally and practically. This skill is vital in building trust, fostering collaboration, and finding solutions that benefit everyone involved.

Example:

A manager deciding on team deadlines uses empathy to recognize that overloading employees might lead to burnout, even if faster results are desired.

Why Empathy Matters in Decision-Making

1. Builds Stronger Relationships:

Empathy fosters trust, making others more likely to support your decisions.

2. Improves Outcomes:

Decisions informed by empathy often address emotional as well as practical needs, leading to more lasting solutions.

3. Reduces Conflict:

Considering others' perspectives helps you avoid misunderstandings and minimize resistance.

Example in Action:

When launching a policy change, a leader who empathizes with employees' concerns about workload may introduce the change gradually to ease the transition.

How to Use Empathy in Decision-Making

1. Listen Actively:

Pay full attention to what others say, without interrupting or formulating a response in your mind.

Example: During a team discussion, listen to concerns about a new project before offering your opinion.

2. Ask Open-Ended Questions:

Invite others to share their thoughts and feelings to gain a deeper understanding of their perspective.

Example: "How do you feel about this change?" or "What challenges are you experiencing?"

3. Consider Emotional Impact:

Ask yourself how your decision might make others feel, and weigh this alongside practical outcomes.

Example: If you're cutting costs in your department, consider how employees will perceive layoffs versus pay cuts, and choose a path that minimizes emotional harm.

4. Acknowledge Others' Feelings:

Show that you value and understand their emotions, even if you don't agree with their perspective.

Example: "I can see why this situation feels overwhelming, and I want to find a way to make it more manageable for you."

Everyday Example of Empathy in Action

Imagine a parent deciding bedtime rules. Instead of enforcing a rigid schedule, they empathize with their child's struggles with night-time fears and allow a compromise, like extra reading time, to ease anxiety while still encouraging rest.

Common Pitfalls in Empathy

1. Assuming Instead of Asking:

Thinking you understand someone's feelings without asking can lead to misjudgements.

2. Letting Empathy Overrule Logic:

While empathy is essential, balance it with practical considerations to avoid unsustainable decisions.

3. Ignoring Boundaries:

Over-empathizing with others can drain your emotional energy. Be mindful of your limits.

Takeaway

Empathy transforms decision-making from a transactional process into a human-centered one. By understanding and considering others' emotions, you can build trust, create better solutions, and make decisions that resonate on a deeper level.

Chapter 43: The Role of Intuition

What Is Intuition?

Intuition is the ability to understand something instinctively, without needing conscious reasoning. Often described as a "gut feeling," it's based on your brain's ability to process patterns, experiences, and subtle cues rapidly, even if you're not aware of it.

Example:

You meet someone at a job interview, and your gut tells you they'd be a great fit for the role — even though you can't immediately pinpoint why.

Why Intuition Matters in Decision-Making

1. Fast Responses in Complex Situations:

Intuition allows you to act quickly when time is limited or data is incomplete.

2. Uses Experience:

Your gut feelings often stem from accumulated knowledge and subconscious pattern recognition.

3. Balances Analysis:

Intuition complements logic by bringing in emotional and instinctive insights that data alone can't provide.

Example in Action:

An experienced doctor might intuitively sense a patient's condition based on subtle, nonverbal cues that aren't obvious in medical tests.

When to Trust Your Intuition

1. When You're Experienced:

Intuition is more reliable when it's based on years of relevant experience.

Example: A skilled chef can instinctively adjust a recipe without measurements, knowing how flavors balance.

2. When the Stakes Are Low:

Gut feelings are a good starting point for smaller decisions, like picking a restaurant or deciding on an outfit.

3. When Data Is Scarce:

In situations where you lack complete information, intuition can fill the gaps and guide you toward action.

4. When You Feel Calm:

Intuition works best when your mind is clear. Emotional overwhelm can distort gut feelings, making them less reliable.

When NOT to Trust Intuition

1. When Bias Is Likely:

Gut instincts can be swayed by cognitive biases, like stereotypes or recent events.

2. When the Decision Is High-Stakes:

For critical choices, such as financial investments or medical decisions, rely on data and expert advice rather than instinct alone.

3. When You're Stressed:

Stress and fatigue can cloud intuition, leading to impulsive or poorly thought-out decisions.

How to Strengthen Your Intuition

1. Reflect on Past Decisions:

Look back at situations where your gut was right or wrong to understand how it works.

2. Learn and Practice:

Intuition improves with experience. The more you engage in a field, the more patterns you'll subconsciously recognize.

3. Pair Intuition with Logic:

Use your gut as a guide but validate it with reasoning or evidence.

Example: If your intuition says a job candidate is a good fit, verify it by checking their qualifications and references.

Everyday Example of Intuition

You're shopping for a gift and spot an item that "feels right" for your friend. Instead of overthinking, you trust your gut, remembering how similar instincts have guided your choices before.

Common Pitfalls in Intuition

1. Confusing Impulse with Intuition:

A gut feeling comes from experience; an impulse is often emotional and fleeting.

2. Ignoring Contradictory Evidence:

Blindly trusting your gut can lead to overlooking facts that contradict your instinct.

3. Overconfidence in Unfamiliar Areas:

Intuition is less reliable in areas where you lack expertise.

Takeaway

Intuition is a powerful tool, especially when paired with experience and logic. By understanding when and how to trust your gut, you can make faster, more confident decisions without sacrificing accuracy.

Chapter 44: Dealing with Decision Fatigue

What Is Decision Fatigue?

Decision Fatigue happens when your mental energy becomes depleted from making too many choices. As the day goes on, the quality of your decisions often declines, leading to impulsive choices, avoidance, or poor judgment.

Example:

After a long day of work, you might order unhealthy takeout instead of cooking a nutritious meal, not because it's the better option, but because you're mentally exhausted from decision-making.

Why Decision Fatigue Can Be Harmful

1. Leads to Poor Choices:

When fatigued, you're more likely to make snap decisions or avoid making a choice altogether.

2. Reduces Willpower:

Decision fatigue can drain your self-control, making it harder to stick to long-term goals.

3. Overloads Your Mind:

Constant decision-making increases stress and diminishes your overall productivity.

Example in Action:

A busy executive juggling multiple meetings and emails might make hasty decisions on important matters just to "clear their plate," only to regret it later.

How to Combat Decision Fatigue

1. Prioritize Important Decisions Early:

Tackle high-stakes decisions when your mind is fresh, usually in the morning or after a break.

Example: If you're deciding on a big purchase, like buying a house, schedule the discussion early in the day.

2. Simplify Routine Choices:

Reduce unnecessary decisions by creating habits or using defaults.

Example: Plan your outfits for the week or meal prep in advance, so you don't waste mental energy on daily small choices.

3. Set Clear Decision Criteria:

Define what you're looking for in advance to streamline your choices.

Example: When choosing a new phone, decide on the key features you need (e.g. price, battery life) to avoid endless comparisons.

4. Take Breaks to Recharge:

Pause between decision-heavy tasks to restore mental clarity.

Example: After a long morning of meetings, take a 15-minute walk to clear your mind before tackling emails.

5. Delegate When Possible:

Share decision-making responsibilities with others to lighten your mental load.

Example: Assign a team member to handle low-priority decisions, freeing you to focus on strategic choices.

Everyday Example of Decision Fatigue

Imagine you've spent hours shopping online for the perfect gift, only to end up buying the first thing you see because you're too tired to think anymore. Planning your shopping in advance or limiting your options can help avoid this spiral.

Common Pitfalls in Managing Decision Fatigue

1. Ignoring Your Limits:

Believing you can make good decisions all day without rest sets you up for failure.

2. Procrastinating:

Postponing decisions to avoid fatigue only creates a backlog of choices, worsening the problem later.

3. Underestimating Small Decisions:

Even minor choices, like deciding what to eat or wear, contribute to mental exhaustion.

Takeaway

Decision fatigue is inevitable, but it doesn't have to derail you. By prioritizing key decisions, simplifying routines, and taking breaks to recharge, you can stay sharp and focused throughout the day.

Chapter 45: Stress-Reduction Techniques

What Is Stress in Decision-Making?

Stress is a natural response to challenges or demands, but when unmanaged, it clouds judgment, narrows your focus, and makes even small decisions feel overwhelming. Prolonged stress can lead to emotional reactions, snap judgments, or indecision.

Example:

Under stress to meet a deadline, you might choose the fastest solution without fully considering its long-term consequences.

Why Stress Reduction Matters in Decision-Making

1. Improves Clarity:

A calm mind is better equipped to evaluate options and anticipate outcomes.

2. Reduces Emotional Reactions:

Stress often triggers impulsive or fear-based decisions.

3. Increases Focus:

Managing stress helps you prioritize tasks and avoid distractions.

Example in Action:

A leader dealing with a team conflict may pause to reduce their stress before mediating, ensuring they approach the issue rationally rather than emotionally.

Stress-Reduction Techniques for Better Decisions

1. Practice Deep Breathing:

Controlled breathing activates your body's relaxation response, reducing stress in the moment.

Example: Inhale for 4 seconds, hold for 4 seconds, and exhale for 4 seconds during a tense meeting to calm yourself.

2. Break Problems Into Smaller Steps:

Overwhelming decisions feel more manageable when divided into smaller, actionable parts.

Example: If you're overwhelmed by a big project, focus first on creating a timeline or completing one small task.

3. Use Visualization:

Picture a positive outcome to reduce anxiety and regain focus.

Example: Before negotiating, visualize yourself confidently presenting your points and reaching a successful agreement.

4. Establish a Routine:

A predictable routine reduces decision overload, leaving you with more mental energy for critical choices.

Example: Starting your day with a set morning ritual (exercise, breakfast, and reviewing priorities) sets a calm tone.

5. Take Physical Breaks:

Exercise, even for a few minutes, releases tension and clears your mind.

Example: A quick walk or stretch between meetings helps reset your focus.

Everyday Example of Stress Reduction

You're juggling multiple errands and start feeling overwhelmed. Instead of pushing through the stress, pause, take a few deep breaths, and reorganize your tasks into a prioritized list. This simple step helps you feel in control and tackle one thing at a time.

1. Ignoring Early Warning Signs:

Waiting until stress becomes overwhelming makes it harder to regain control.

2. Avoiding the Problem:

Distracting yourself from stress without addressing its source only delays the inevitable.

3. Relying on Unhealthy Coping Mechanisms:

Turning to habits like overeating or procrastinating might provide short-term relief but worsens stress in the long run.

Takeaway

Stress is unavoidable, but it doesn't have to derail your decision-making. By practicing simple, effective stress-reduction techniques, you can maintain clarity and focus even in high-pressure situations.

Chapter 46: The Pause Principle

What Is the Pause Principle?

The Pause Principle is the idea that stepping back and delaying a decision — even briefly — can lead to better outcomes. When emotions run high or the stakes feel overwhelming, pausing provides the mental space needed to reflect, gather information, and regain perspective.

Example:

Before responding to a heated email, pausing for a few hours helps you craft a calm, professional reply rather than reacting impulsively.

Why Pausing Matters in Decision-Making

1. Reduces Emotional Reactions:

Waiting allows intense emotions like anger, fear, or excitement to settle, preventing impulsive choices.

2. Creates Time for Clarity:

Pausing helps you process complex information, weigh options, and consider long-term consequences.

3. Enhances Perspective:

A break from decision-making can reveal solutions or angles you hadn't considered before.

Example:

A business owner deciding whether to accept an aggressive partnership offer might pause for a day to consult mentors and review the terms with fresh eyes.

How to Practice the Pause Principle

1. Acknowledge the Need to Pause:

Recognize when you're feeling rushed or emotionally overwhelmed, and give yourself permission to wait.

Example: If you feel pressured to decide during a sales pitch, tell the salesperson, "I'll need time to think about it."

2. Set a Specific Timeline:

Pausing doesn't mean procrastinating. Decide how long you'll wait and what you'll do in the meantime.

Example: If you're unsure about accepting a job offer, take 24 hours to reflect and gather more information.

3. Engage in a Calming Activity:

Use the pause to clear your mind, such as taking a walk, meditating, or journaling your thoughts.

Example: If you're stuck on a creative decision, a short break away from your workspace can spark new ideas.

4. Revisit the Decision with a Fresh Perspective:

After the pause, re-evaluate the situation with a clearer, more objective mindset.

Everyday Example of the Pause Principle

Imagine you're deciding whether to make an expensive purchase online. Instead of clicking "Buy Now" immediately, pause for 24 hours to consider whether you truly need the item. Often, the urgency fades, and you can make a more rational decision.

Common Pitfalls in Pausing

1. Confusing Pausing with Procrastination:

Pausing is intentional and productive, while procrastination avoids decision-making altogether.

2. Pausing Indefinitely:

Setting no deadline for your decision can lead to analysis paralysis.

3. Using Pauses to Avoid Responsibility:

Overusing pauses to delay tough choices prevents progress.

Takeaway

The Pause Principle is a powerful tool for decision-making. By taking intentional breaks when you feel rushed or overwhelmed, you gain clarity, avoid impulsive errors, and make choices with greater confidence.

Chapter 47: Handling Regret

What Is Regret in Decision-Making?

Regret is the emotional pain of wishing you'd made a different choice. It's a natural part of decision-making but can become a mental weight that stops you from moving forward. Learning how to handle regret allows you to grow from past experiences instead of being trapped by them.

Example:

You regret not applying for a job that seemed intimidating at the time. Instead of dwelling on it, you use the experience to motivate yourself to seize similar opportunities in the future.

Why Handling Regret Matters

1. Frees You from the Past:

Learning to release regret allows you to focus on the present and future.

2. Encourages Growth:

Reflecting on regret helps you identify lessons and improve future decisions.

3. Prevents Decision Paralysis:

Fear of future regret can stop you from taking necessary risks. By managing regret effectively, you're more willing to make bold choices.

Example in Action:

After regretting a failed investment, a person revises their financial strategy instead of avoiding investments altogether.

How to Handle Regret Gracefully

1. Acknowledge Your Feelings:

Denying regret only prolongs its emotional impact. Accept your feelings to begin moving forward.

Example: Instead of suppressing regret over ending a relationship, admit, "I feel sad about my decision, but I made the best choice with what I knew then."

2. Reframe the Experience:

Focus on what you gained or learned from the situation.

Example: "I didn't get the promotion, but the preparation helped me improve my skills for the next opportunity."

3. Take Action to Improve:

Use regret as motivation to make better decisions in the future.

Example: If you regret skipping a networking event, resolve to attend the next one and prepare in advance.

4. Practice Self-Compassion:

Treat yourself with kindness instead of harsh criticism.

Example: Remind yourself, "I'm human, and mistakes are part of learning."

Everyday Example of Handling Regret

You regret buying an expensive gadget that you barely use. Instead of feeling stuck in the past, you sell it online, recover part of your money, and vow to research more thoroughly before future purchases.

Common Pitfalls in Handling Regret

1. Dwelling on "What Ifs":

Constantly imagining alternate outcomes traps you in a cycle of second-guessing.

2. Letting Regret Define You:

Seeing yourself as a "failure" because of one choice undermines your confidence.

3. Avoiding Risks Entirely:

Fear of future regret can lead to overly cautious decisions, stifling growth.

Takeaway

Regret is a powerful teacher if you let it be. By acknowledging your feelings, reframing your experiences, and focusing on growth, you can move forward gracefully and make peace with past decisions.

Chapter 48: Mindfulness Practices

What Is Mindfulness in Decision-Making?

Mindfulness is the practice of bringing your full attention to the present moment, free of judgment or distraction. In decision-making, mindfulness helps you focus on what matters, process information clearly, and resist impulsive reactions. It sharpens your awareness of both your thoughts and emotions, ensuring your choices align with your goals and values.

Example:

When faced with a tough choice, practicing mindfulness allows you to stay calm, assess the options objectively, and avoid being swayed by fleeting emotions.

Why Mindfulness Matters in Decision-Making

1. Increases Focus:

By tuning out distractions, you can fully engage with the decision at hand.

2. Reduces Emotional Reactivity:

Mindfulness helps you observe emotions without letting them cloud your judgment.

3. Enhances Clarity:

It allows you to view situations objectively, free from assumptions or mental clutter.

Example:

A leader preparing for a critical meeting uses mindfulness to calm pre-presentation nerves, enabling them to think clearly and respond thoughtfully.

How to Practice Mindfulness for Better Decisions

1. Pause and Breathe:

Take a few deep breaths to ground yourself before tackling a decision.

Example: When overwhelmed by competing priorities, pause for a minute to breathe deeply, reducing stress and improving focus.

2. Focus on the Present Moment:

Bring your attention fully to the task at hand, avoiding the urge to multitask.

Example: If reviewing a proposal, set aside distractions like emails or phone notifications to give it your full attention.

3. Acknowledge Your Thoughts:

Notice any mental distractions, biases, or emotions, but don't let them control you.

Example: If you feel anxious about a decision, acknowledge the anxiety without acting on it impulsively.

4. Use Guided Mindfulness Exercises:

Practices like body scans, meditation apps, or mindful walking can help train your focus over time.

Example: Spend 5–10 minutes daily focusing on your breathing to build mindfulness as a habit.

Everyday Example of Mindfulness

You're deciding whether to accept a last-minute invitation to an event. Instead of rushing to respond, you take a moment to focus on how the decision aligns with your priorities. Mindfulness helps you choose based on what matters most, rather than social pressure.

Common Pitfalls in Mindfulness Practices

1. Expecting Instant Results:

Mindfulness is a skill that improves with consistent practice, not a quick fix.

2. Overcomplicating the Process:

You don't need elaborate techniques — even a minute of focused breathing can make a difference.

3. Using Mindfulness to Avoid Action:

Reflection is important, but it should lead to thoughtful decisions, not endless contemplation.

Takeaway

Mindfulness empowers you to approach decisions with clarity, focus, and calm. By grounding yourself in the present moment and observing your thoughts without judgment, you can make choices that reflect your true priorities and values.

Chapter 49: Cultivating Resilience

What Is Resilience in Decision-Making?

Resilience is the ability to recover from setbacks, adapt to change, and keep moving forward after failure. In decision-making, resilience means learning from mistakes, staying persistent in the face of challenges, and maintaining confidence in your ability to make progress.

Example:

After a failed product launch, a resilient entrepreneur analyzes what went wrong, adjusts their strategy, and tries again with a new approach.

Why Resilience Matters in Decision-Making

1. Encourages Growth:

Resilience helps you view failure as a stepping stone rather than an endpoint.

2. Builds Confidence:

Knowing you can recover from setbacks makes you more willing to take calculated risks.

3. Improves Long-Term Success:

Resilience allows you to stay committed to your goals, even when facing temporary obstacles.

Example:

A student who fails an exam doesn't give up but instead studies harder, seeks help, and improves their performance on the next test.

How to Cultivate Resilience

1. Reframe Failure as Feedback:

Treat every setback as an opportunity to learn and improve.

Example: Instead of thinking, "I'm bad at negotiating," reflect on what you can do differently next time.

2. Focus on What You Can Control:

Let go of factors outside your influence and channel your energy into actionable steps.

Example: If a job interview doesn't go well, focus on preparing for the next one rather than dwelling on the outcome.

3. Build a Support Network:

Surround yourself with people who encourage and challenge you to keep going.

Example: Share your struggles with mentors, friends, or colleagues who can provide perspective and advice.

4. Practice Self-Compassion:

Be kind to yourself during difficult times and remind yourself that setbacks are part of the process.

Example: Instead of harshly criticizing yourself for a mistake, say, "I'm learning and growing through this experience."

Everyday Example of Resilience

You start a fitness routine but miss a few workouts during a busy week. Instead of giving up entirely, you remind yourself that progress isn't perfect and get back on track the next week.

Common Pitfalls in Building Resilience

1. Dwelling on Failure:

Excessively focusing on what went wrong prevents you from moving forward.

2. Ignoring Emotional Recovery:

Resilience isn't just about action; it also involves processing emotions and regaining mental balance.

3. Expecting Instant Progress:

Resilience is built over time through consistent effort and reflection.

Takeaway

Resilience is your greatest ally in decision-making. By embracing failure as part of growth, focusing on what you can control, and nurturing self-compassion, you can bounce back stronger and make better choices in the future.

Chapter 50: Making Peace with Uncertainty

What Is Uncertainty in Decision-Making?

Uncertainty is the unavoidable reality that no decision comes with absolute guarantees. The future is inherently unpredictable, but learning to accept and navigate uncertainty allows you to make progress despite the unknown.

Example:

When choosing to switch careers, uncertainty about the outcome may feel daunting. However, embracing the unknown creates opportunities for growth and new experiences.

Why Embracing Uncertainty Matters

1. Encourages Action:

Waiting for perfect information leads to stagnation. Accepting uncertainty helps you move forward.

2. Increases Flexibility:

Acknowledging the unknown allows you to adapt as circumstances change.

3. Reduces Fear:

Making peace with uncertainty reduces anxiety and empowers you to focus on what you can control.

Example:

An entrepreneur launching a startup embraces the uncertainty of market demand but prepares to pivot based on customer feedback.

How to Make Peace with Uncertainty

1. Focus on Probabilities, Not Guarantees:

Weigh the likelihood of outcomes and act based on the most informed choice.

Example: If you're unsure about investing, consider the risks and potential returns, then make a calculated decision.

2. Plan for Multiple Scenarios:

Prepare backup plans to address various possible outcomes.

Example: When planning an event, consider how you'd adapt to rain or other unexpected changes.

3. Build Confidence in Adaptability:

Remind yourself of past challenges you've overcome, reinforcing your ability to handle uncertainty.

Example: Reflect on a time when you thrived despite not knowing the full picture upfront.

4. Take Incremental Steps:

Break big decisions into smaller, manageable actions to reduce the pressure of uncertainty.

Example: Instead of committing to a major move all at once, visit the new city and test the waters first.

Everyday Example of Embracing Uncertainty

You're trying a new recipe for a dinner party, unsure how it will turn out. By focusing on the process, enjoying the experience, and having a backup dish ready, you reduce anxiety about the outcome.

Common Pitfalls in Handling Uncertainty

1. Paralysis by Analysis:

Overthinking every variable can prevent you from taking action.

2. Seeking Absolute Certainty:

Waiting for perfect clarity wastes time and delays progress.

3. Underpreparing for Risks:

While embracing uncertainty is important, ignoring potential challenges can lead to avoidable setbacks.

Takeaway

Uncertainty is a constant in decision-making, but it doesn't have to be paralyzing. By focusing on probabilities, planning flexibly, and building confidence in your ability to adapt, you can embrace the unknown as a source of opportunity rather than fear.

Part VI: Group and Team Decision-Making

In this section, you'll learn techniques for turning group dynamics into an advantage rather than a challenge, ensuring fair, informed, and effective decisions.

Chapter 51: Consensus-Building

What Is Consensus-Building?

Consensus-building is the process of finding common ground among a group with differing opinions. It's not about forcing complete agreement or compromising on every issue but creating a solution that everyone can support and feels invested in.

Example:

When planning a team event, consensus might mean choosing a venue that's not everyone's first choice but meets key needs like accessibility and cost.

Why Consensus-Building Matters

1. Increases Buy-In:

When people feel heard and included, they're more likely to support the final decision.

2. Improves Decision Quality:

By considering multiple perspectives, you're less likely to miss important factors.

3. Reduces Conflict:

A collaborative approach minimizes resentment and fosters teamwork.

Example in Action:

A city council uses consensus-building to decide on a budget by inviting input from all stakeholders and addressing key concerns transparently.

How to Build Consensus

1. Define Shared Goals:

Start by identifying the group's common objectives to keep discussions focused.

Example: If your team is choosing a project management tool, agree that the priority is ease of use and compatibility with existing systems.

2. Encourage Open Dialogue:

Create a safe space where everyone feels comfortable sharing their views, even if they differ from the majority.

Example: Use a round-robin format to ensure quieter members have a chance to speak.

3. Identify Key Areas of Agreement and Disagreement:

Highlight shared opinions and focus discussions on resolving specific points of contention.

Example: If most team members agree on a timeline but differ on the budget, spend time aligning expectations around costs.

4. Use a Facilitator:

Appoint someone to guide the discussion, keep it on track, and ensure everyone's voice is heard.

Example: A neutral facilitator can summarize points and mediate when discussions become heated.

Everyday Example of Consensus-Building

Your family is deciding where to go on vacation. Instead of letting one person decide, everyone lists their priorities. Through discussion, you agree on a destination that includes activities everyone can enjoy, like hiking and sightseeing.

Common Pitfalls in Consensus-Building

1. Forcing Agreement:

Seeking unanimous approval can lead to frustration or watered-down decisions.

2. Ignoring Minority Voices:

Rushing to agreement may silence valuable dissenting opinions.

3. Taking Too Long:

Endless discussions can delay decisions. Set clear timelines for reaching consensus.

Takeaway

Consensus-building aligns diverse opinions. By fostering open dialogue, focusing on shared goals, and resolving disagreements collaboratively, you can turn differences into a strength.

Chapter 52: Avoiding Power Dynamics

What Are Power Dynamics in Group Decisions?

Power dynamics refer to the influence that authority, status, or personality can have on a group's decision-making process. When unchecked, power imbalances can silence important perspectives or push the group toward biased outcomes.

Example:

In a team meeting, a manager's strong opinion might discourage others from sharing alternative ideas, leading to a decision based on authority rather than collaboration.

Why Avoiding Power Dynamics Matters

1. Ensures Equal Contribution:

Fair processes encourage everyone to share their ideas, leading to richer discussions.

2. Reduces Bias:

Decisions are more objective when they're not dominated by one person's influence.

3. Builds Trust:

Teams that feel valued and respected are more engaged and collaborative.

Example:

A project leader who invites quiet team members to share their input ensures that decisions reflect diverse perspectives, not just the loudest voice in the room.

How to Avoid Power Dynamics

1. Use a Neutral Facilitator:

Appoint someone to lead discussions impartially, ensuring no single voice dominates.

Example: A facilitator might say, "Let's hear from those who haven't spoken yet."

2. Encourage Anonymous Input:

Use surveys, suggestion boxes, or online tools to collect ideas without revealing names.

Example: When deciding on a new workplace policy, an anonymous poll can ensure that employees feel safe sharing honest opinions.

3. Rotate Leadership Roles:

Share responsibility for leading discussions to prevent hierarchical influence.

Example: Each team member takes turns running weekly meetings to create a more balanced dynamic.

4. Create Clear Guidelines:

Establish rules for discussions, such as limiting interruptions or giving everyone equal speaking time.

Example: Set a timer to ensure each participant has a chance to speak during brainstorming sessions.

Everyday Example of Avoiding Power Dynamics

At a family gathering, one person usually decides what's for dinner. To make the process fairer, everyone writes down a meal idea, and the group votes anonymously, ensuring all preferences are considered equally.

Common Pitfalls in Avoiding Power Dynamics

1. Allowing Dominance:

Without clear guidelines, strong personalities or authority figures may still control the discussion.

2. Neglecting Quiet Voices:

Introverted or junior members may hesitate to speak unless actively encouraged.

3. Overcompensating for Authority:

Trying too hard to suppress leaders' input can exclude valuable expertise.

Takeaway

Avoiding power dynamics ensures that decisions are fair, collaborative, and representative of the group's collective wisdom. By creating equal opportunities to contribute and neutralizing imbalances, you empower teams to reach better outcomes together.

Chapter 53: The Wisdom of Crowds

What Is the Wisdom of Crowds?

The Wisdom of Crowds is the concept that groups of diverse individuals, working together or independently, can often make better decisions than a single expert. By pooling their varied knowledge, experiences, and perspectives, groups can identify innovative solutions and avoid blind spots.

Example:

In a business setting, a diverse team brainstorming ideas for a marketing campaign may collectively generate more creative and effective strategies than a single marketing expert working alone.

Why the Wisdom of Crowds Matters

1. Taps Into Diverse Perspectives:

A wide range of viewpoints uncovers insights that individuals might miss.

2. Reduces Individual Bias:

Groups dilute the influence of personal biases, leading to more balanced decisions.

3. Leads to Better Predictions:

Aggregating estimates from multiple people often results in more accurate forecasts.

Example:

Crowdsourcing platforms like Kickstarter rely on the wisdom of the crowd to identify which creative projects resonate most with potential backers.

How to Leverage the Wisdom of Crowds

1. Foster Diversity:

Include people with different backgrounds, skills, and perspectives to enrich group discussions.

Example: When forming a task force, invite members from different departments to provide varied expertise.

2. Encourage Independent Input:

Collect individual opinions before group discussions to avoid the influence of groupthink.

Example: Before a strategy meeting, ask team members to submit their ideas anonymously.

3. Aggregate Insights Systematically:

Use structured methods to combine group input, such as voting, ranking, or statistical analysis.

Example: When forecasting sales, collect estimates from all team members and calculate the average.

4. Focus on Problem-Solving:

Direct the group's energy toward clearly defined goals to ensure productive collaboration.

Example: Provide a specific question like, "What features should we prioritize in the next product release?" rather than vague prompts.

Everyday Example of the Wisdom of Crowds

Imagine planning a party. Instead of deciding everything yourself, you ask a group of friends to suggest venues, menus, and activities. Their combined input helps you create a more enjoyable event than you could have planned alone.

Common Pitfalls in the Wisdom of Crowds

1. Ignoring Diversity:

Groups that lack varied perspectives are more likely to fall into groupthink or confirmation bias.

2. Overvaluing Majority Opinions:

Majority opinions aren't always correct — ensure minority views are considered.

3. Failing to Structure Collaboration:

Without clear processes, group discussions can become chaotic or unproductive.

Takeaway

The Wisdom of Crowds highlights the power of collective intelligence in decision-making. By fostering diversity, encouraging independent input, and structuring group processes, you can harness the strengths of collaboration for smarter, more balanced outcomes.

Chapter 54: The Delphi Technique

What Is the Delphi Technique?

The Delphi Technique is a structured, iterative method for solving complex problems or making decisions. It involves gathering input from a panel of experts through multiple rounds of anonymous feedback and refining the group's responses until a consensus emerges. This process minimizes the influence of dominant personalities and encourages thoughtful collaboration.

Example:

A city planning team might use the Delphi Technique to gather expert opinions on how to address traffic congestion, refining proposals through multiple feedback rounds.

Why the Delphi Technique Matters

1. Encourages Objective Input:

Anonymity ensures that ideas are evaluated on their merits rather than the status of the person suggesting them.

2. Facilitates Informed Consensus:

Iterative feedback refines ideas and builds agreement among diverse experts.

3. Addresses Complex Issues:

The technique is ideal for tackling problems with no clear or straightforward solutions.

Example:

Healthcare organizations use the Delphi Technique to develop treatment guidelines by consulting multiple specialists and refining recommendations through feedback rounds.

How to Use the Delphi Technique

1. Select a Panel of Experts:

Choose participants with relevant knowledge and varied perspectives to ensure balanced input.

Example: For a technology upgrade, include IT professionals, end-users, and budget analysts.

2. Use Anonymous Surveys:

Conduct multiple rounds of anonymous questionnaires to collect opinions and solutions.

Example: In the first round, ask for open-ended suggestions. In subsequent rounds, refine and rank these ideas.

3. Iterate Feedback:

Share summarized responses after each round to guide further refinement.

Example: Present a narrowed list of traffic solutions to the panel, asking them to rank or critique the options.

4. Achieve Consensus:

Continue the process until the group reaches a consensus or a well-defined set of recommendations.

Example: After several rounds, the city planning team agrees on prioritizing public transit improvements.

Everyday Example of the Delphi Technique

Imagine organizing a neighborhood event. You ask residents for anonymous suggestions on activities, then narrow the list and gather feedback through follow-up surveys. This process ensures that the event reflects the community's collective preferences.

Common Pitfalls in the Delphi Technique

1. Choosing the Wrong Experts:

Including participants without relevant expertise can dilute the quality of feedback.

2. Skipping Iterations:

Rushing the process undermines the value of refinement and consensus-building.

3. Overcomplicating the Process:

Too many rounds or overly complex questions can lead to participant fatigue.

Takeaway

The Delphi Technique is a powerful tool for collaborative problem-solving, especially when dealing with complex or uncertain issues. By structuring feedback, fostering objectivity, and refining ideas iteratively, you can guide groups toward informed, effective decisions.

Chapter 55: Role Assignment

What Is Role Assignment in Decision-Making?

Role assignment is the process of clearly defining each person's responsibilities within a group. It ensures that everyone knows their specific tasks, preventing duplication of effort, confusion, or gaps in execution. Clear role assignment is essential for both efficient decision-making and effective follow-through.

Example:

In a product launch, one team member might handle marketing, another logistics, and a third customer support. Clear assignments ensure each aspect of the project is covered without overlap or confusion.

Why Role Assignment Matters

1. Enhances Accountability:

When roles are clearly defined, team members understand what's expected of them and take ownership of their tasks.

2. Prevents Confusion:

Role clarity eliminates misunderstandings about who's responsible for what, ensuring smoother collaboration.

3. Increases Efficiency:

Assigning specific roles helps the group focus on individual strengths, streamlining decision-making and execution.

Example:

During an event planning meeting, assigning roles like "Budget Manager" and "Venue Coordinator" ensures that key tasks are handled without redundancy or missed deadlines.

How to Assign Roles Effectively

1. Identify Key Tasks:

Break the project or decision into its major components, such as research, communication, and implementation.

Example: In a marketing campaign, tasks might include content creation, data analysis, and ad placement.

2. Match Roles to Strengths:

Assign tasks based on each person's skills, experience, and preferences to maximize effectiveness.

Example: If someone is detail-oriented, assign them the task of proofreading documents.

3. Clearly Communicate Expectations:

Define each role's responsibilities and deadlines to ensure everyone understands their part.

Example: "As the Research Lead, you'll collect and summarize competitor data by next Friday."

4. Provide Support and Flexibility:

Encourage collaboration and adaptability, allowing team members to step in for each other if needed.

Example: If the Logistics Manager is overwhelmed, another member might assist with vendor coordination.

Everyday Example of Role Assignment

Your family is organizing a holiday dinner. To simplify planning, one person handles the shopping list, another cooks, and a third decorates. By dividing tasks based on each person's strengths, the process becomes more organized and enjoyable.

Common Pitfalls in Role Assignment

1. Assigning Roles Arbitrarily:

Ignoring individual strengths and interests can lead to poor performance and frustration.

2. Failing to Communicate:

Unclear roles often result in duplicate efforts or overlooked tasks.

3. Overloading One Person:

Uneven task distribution can cause resentment or burnout.

Takeaway

Role assignment brings structure, clarity, and accountability to group decision-making. By matching tasks to individual strengths and communicating expectations clearly, you can ensure smoother collaboration and more effective outcomes.

"LET'S FIND A WAY TO BALANCE THESE CONCERNS."

Chapter 56: Conflict Resolution Skills

What Are Conflict Resolution Skills?

Conflict resolution involves addressing disagreements constructively to reach a solution that respects all parties involved. In group decision-making, conflicts can arise from differing priorities, opinions, or values. The goal isn't to avoid conflict but to navigate it in a way that strengthens the group's collaboration.

Example:

Two team members might disagree about how to allocate a budget. Effective conflict resolution ensures that both perspectives are heard, leading to a fair compromise.

Why Conflict Resolution Matters

1. Strengthens Relationships:

Addressing conflicts openly fosters trust and mutual respect.

2. Leads to Better Decisions:

Healthy disagreements can uncover blind spots and lead to more innovative solutions.

3. Prevents Escalation:

Resolving conflicts early prevents misunderstandings from growing into larger issues.

Example:

A project manager mediates between two designers who disagree on branding elements, encouraging collaboration to create a unified design that blends their ideas.

How to Resolve Conflicts Productively

1. Listen Actively:

Focus on understanding each person's perspective without interrupting or judging.

Example: Repeat back key points to show you're listening: "So, you're concerned about the timeline being too short?"

2. Stay Objective:

Focus on the issue, not the individuals involved, to avoid personal attacks or defensiveness.

Example: Frame the conflict as a shared challenge: "How can we balance speed with quality?"

3. Encourage Open Dialogue:

Create a safe space for everyone to express their thoughts and feelings honestly.

Example: "Let's take turns sharing our perspectives so we can fully understand each other's concerns."

4. Seek Common Ground:

Identify shared goals or values to build a foundation for compromise.

Example: "We all agree that delivering a high-quality product is the priority, so let's focus on how to achieve that together."

5. Propose and Evaluate Solutions:

Brainstorm possible resolutions, weighing the pros and cons of each.

Example: "What if we adjust the deadline slightly to allow for additional quality checks?"

Everyday Example of Conflict Resolution

Two roommates argue about household chores. By discussing their expectations and creating a clear schedule, they resolve the issue and improve their living arrangement.

Common Pitfalls in Conflict Resolution

1. Avoiding the Issue:

Ignoring conflicts often makes them worse, as frustrations build over time.

2. Taking Sides:

In group settings, biased mediation can worsen tensions.

3. Focusing on Winning:

Viewing conflict as a competition prevents collaborative problem-solving.

Takeaway

Conflict is an inevitable part of group decision-making, but it doesn't have to be destructive. By fostering open communication, focusing on shared goals, and approaching disagreements with respect, you can turn conflicts into opportunities for growth and stronger collaboration.

> If we go with **Option A**, it costs more but gets faster results.

> And **Option B** is cheaper, but it could delay the project. Let's weigh the long-term benefits.

Chapter 57: Decision Mapping for Teams

What Is Decision Mapping?

Decision mapping is a visual tool that outlines the choices, consequences, and potential outcomes involved in a decision. For teams, it provides a structured way to organize ideas, clarify roles, and ensure everyone understands the bigger picture. It's especially helpful for breaking down complex problems into manageable parts.

Example:

When planning a company expansion, a decision map might include branches for location options, costs, potential risks, and long-term benefits, helping the team evaluate all factors systematically.

Why Decision Mapping Matters

1. Improves Clarity:

A visual representation helps teams see the connections between choices and outcomes, reducing confusion.

2. Encourages Collaboration:

Mapping decisions ensures all team members can contribute their ideas and understand the logic behind decisions.

3. Simplifies Complexity:

Breaking a big decision into smaller components makes it easier to analyze and discuss.

Example:

A nonprofit team uses decision mapping to plan a fundraising event, outlining choices for venue, marketing strategies, and ticket pricing, along with their potential impacts.

How to Use Decision Mapping in Teams

1. Start with the Main Question:

Write the central decision you need to make in the middle of the map.

Example: "Which software should we adopt for project management?"

2. Identify Key Choices:

Branch out from the central question with the major options or pathways available.

Example: Branches might include "Tool A," "Tool B," and "Tool C."

3. List Pros, Cons, and Consequences:

Under each branch, map out the benefits, drawbacks, and potential outcomes of each choice.

Example: For "Tool A," list factors like cost, ease of use, and compatibility with existing systems.

4. Incorporate Team Input:

Invite all team members to suggest ideas or identify risks, adding their contributions to the map.

Example: Someone might point out hidden costs or opportunities you hadn't considered.

5. Evaluate and Decide:

Use the map to compare options, prioritize key factors, and reach a consensus.

Everyday Example of Decision Mapping

You're planning a family vacation. A decision map might include branches for destinations, travel costs, activities, and weather conditions, helping everyone agree on the best option based on shared priorities.

Common Pitfalls in Decision Mapping

1. Overloading the Map:

Including too much detail can make the map overwhelming and counterproductive.

2. Skipping Collaboration:

If only one person creates the map, it may miss important perspectives.

3. Focusing Only on Short-Term Outcomes:

Ensure the map includes long-term implications to provide a complete picture.

Takeaway

Decision mapping turns complex choices into clear, visual pathways. By organizing options, consequences, and feedback in one place, teams can collaborate more effectively and make decisions with confidence and transparency.

Chapter 58: Encouraging Constructive Dissent

What Is Constructive Dissent?

Constructive dissent is the practice of encouraging team members to voice disagreements or alternative ideas in a respectful, productive way. It challenges groupthink, sparks innovation, and ensures all perspectives are considered before reaching a decision.

Example:

During a product design meeting, one team member points out potential flaws in a proposed feature, leading to a better alternative that saves time and resources.

Why Constructive Dissent Matters

1. Prevents Groupthink:

Encouraging dissent ensures decisions aren't made just to maintain harmony, leading to better outcomes.

2. Uncovers Blind Spots:

Alternative viewpoints can reveal risks or opportunities the group might otherwise overlook.

3. Fosters Creativity:

Disagreement forces the team to think critically and explore new ideas.

Example in Action:

A marketing team planning a campaign avoids a costly mistake when one member questions the target audience's preferences, prompting a reevaluation of their approach.

How to Encourage Constructive Dissent

1. Create a Safe Space:

Foster a culture where dissent is welcomed and respected, not punished or dismissed.

Example: "All ideas are valid here, and differing opinions are encouraged."

2. Frame Dissent as Collaboration:

Position disagreements as a way to improve the group's ideas, not as personal attacks.

Example: "That's a good point — let's explore how we can address it."

3. Model Dissent as a Leader:

Leaders should ask critical questions or play devil's advocate to show that dissent is valued.

Example: "What's the strongest argument against this idea?"

4. Focus on Evidence, Not Emotion:

Encourage team members to support their dissent with data or logic rather than personal preferences.

Example: "I disagree with this budget allocation because past campaigns showed better ROI with a smaller spend on social ads."

Everyday Example of Constructive Dissent

During a group project at school, one member points out that the team's proposed solution doesn't fully address the assignment criteria. This sparks a discussion that leads to a more effective final plan.

Common Pitfalls in Constructive Dissent

1. Ignoring Dissent:

Dismissing alternative ideas discourages participation and weakens team trust.

2. Confusing Dissent with Conflict:

Disagreement doesn't mean disrespect — focus on the idea, not the person.

3. Overemphasizing Consensus:

Pushing for agreement too quickly can stifle important feedback.

Takeaway

Constructive dissent turns disagreement into a powerful decision-making tool. By creating a culture that values alternative perspectives and critical thinking, teams can avoid groupthink, uncover better solutions, and make stronger choices together.

Chapter 59: Combating Group Polarization

What Is Group Polarization?

Group polarization occurs when group discussions push members toward more extreme positions than they initially held. Instead of reaching balanced decisions, group dynamics amplify shared emotions, beliefs, or biases, leading to overly risky or overly cautious outcomes.

Example:

In a team debate about a marketing strategy, a group that initially favored a modest budget might escalate toward cutting it drastically after reinforcing one another's fears about overspending.

Why Group Polarization Matters

1. Skews Decision-Making:

Extreme group opinions often overlook important nuances or alternative options.

2. Increases Risk:

Polarization can push groups toward decisions that are too risky or overly conservative, depending on the shared mindset.

3. Undermines Collaboration:

Polarized groups may alienate dissenting voices, reducing the quality of the final decision.

Example:

A group of investors initially hesitant about a project might become overly risk-averse, deciding against it altogether after amplifying each other's doubts — even if the project has significant potential.

How to Combat Group Polarization

1. Encourage Diverse Perspectives:

Actively invite opinions that challenge the group's dominant view to introduce balance.

Example: Ask, "What would someone with a different perspective say about this decision?"

2. Focus on Evidence, Not Emotion:

Redirect discussions toward data and facts rather than emotional or subjective arguments.

Example: "Let's review the market analysis again before we decide to cut the budget completely."

3. Appoint a Devil's Advocate:

Assign someone to argue the opposite side of the group's leaning to test assumptions.

Example: In a meeting where the group leans heavily toward risk, a devil's advocate might say, "What happens if we overinvest and the market doesn't respond?"

4. Break Into Smaller Groups:

Divide the group to discuss the issue separately and then compare findings to reduce groupthink.

Example: Two subgroups might analyze different strategies, bringing their perspectives back to the full team for comparison.

5. Revisit Initial Positions:

Ask members to reflect on their original opinions and consider whether the group's shift is rational or emotional.

Example: "Is this conclusion consistent with the preferences we had when we started, or have we drifted too far?"

Everyday Example of Group Polarization

During a neighborhood meeting, initial concerns about traffic from a proposed park lead to extreme objections, like canceling the project altogether. A balanced discussion that focuses on traffic management solutions might help the group return to moderation.

Common Pitfalls in Combating Group Polarization

1. Ignoring Minority Opinions:

Dismissing alternative views strengthens the group's extreme stance.

2. Letting Emotions Drive Decisions:

High emotions, like fear or excitement, fuel polarization.

3. Failing to Intervene:

Allowing the group to spiral without redirection results in less rational decisions.

Takeaway

Group polarization can distort decision-making and lead to extreme outcomes. By fostering diverse perspectives, grounding discussions in evidence, and encouraging critical thinking, you can guide groups back to balanced, well-informed choices.

Chapter 60: Accountability in Groups

What Is Accountability in Group Decision-Making?

Accountability ensures that group decisions translate into action by assigning clear responsibilities and tracking progress. It's not enough to agree on a decision; each team member must commit to their role in executing it, and the group must monitor results to stay on track.

Example:

After deciding to launch a new product, the team assigns tasks like market research, product development, and marketing to specific members, with deadlines and regular check-ins to ensure accountability.

Why Accountability Matters

1. Ensures Execution:

Accountability bridges the gap between decision-making and action, preventing good ideas from stalling.

2. Builds Trust:

When everyone fulfills their responsibilities, the team develops mutual respect and confidence.

3. Improves Outcomes:

Regular progress reviews allow teams to identify and address obstacles early.

Example:

A charity planning a fundraiser assigns one member to handle sponsorship outreach and another to manage event logistics. Regular updates ensure tasks are completed on time.

How to Foster Accountability in Groups

1. Assign Specific Roles and Deadlines:

Clearly define who is responsible for each task and set realistic timelines.

Example: "Sam will finalize the vendor contract by Monday, and Alex will prepare the budget report by Friday."

2. Track Progress Regularly:

Schedule check-ins to review progress, address challenges, and maintain momentum.

Example: Weekly meetings might include updates on each team member's progress and upcoming tasks.

3. Document Decisions and Responsibilities:

Record group decisions and share them with everyone to ensure clarity and transparency.

Example: After each meeting, send a summary that lists tasks, owners, and deadlines.

4. Celebrate Success and Address Gaps:

Acknowledge completed tasks while addressing delays or issues constructively.

Example: "Great job on the presentation, Maria! Let's discuss how we can support Liam in completing his report on time."

5. Use Tools for Accountability:

Leverage project management tools like Trello or Asana to assign tasks, set deadlines, and monitor progress.

Everyday Example of Accountability

In a family setting, deciding to renovate the kitchen requires accountability. One member might be tasked with getting quotes, another with choosing materials, and another with setting the budget. Regular updates ensure the project stays on track.

Common Pitfalls in Group Accountability

1. Vague Assignments:

Failing to specify who is responsible for what leads to confusion and inaction.

2. Lack of Follow-Up:

Without progress checks, tasks may be delayed or forgotten.

3. Blaming Without Support:

Criticizing team members for missed tasks without offering solutions undermines morale.

Takeaway

Accountability is the foundation of effective group decision-making and execution. By assigning clear responsibilities, tracking progress, and fostering a culture of support, teams can ensure that their decisions lead to meaningful, actionable outcomes.

Part VII: Strategic Thinking for Long-Term Success

Big decisions require big-picture thinking. Strategic decision-making isn't just about solving today's problems — it's about anticipating tomorrow's challenges and opportunities. This section equips you with tools to plan for the future, weigh probabilities, and take decisive action when the moment is right.

Chapter 61: Game Theory Basics

What Is Game Theory?

Game theory is the study of strategic interactions where the outcome of your choices depends on the actions of others. It's about thinking beyond your immediate goals and predicting how others will respond to your decisions.

Example:

In negotiations, offering a fair proposal can influence the other party to cooperate rather than compete, leading to a win-win outcome.

Why Game Theory Matters

1. Improves Strategic Thinking:

Game theory forces you to think several steps ahead, like in a chess match.

2. Prepares for Countermoves:

Understanding others' motivations helps you anticipate and prepare for their reactions.

3. Encourages Collaboration:

Identifying mutual benefits reduces unnecessary conflict and creates shared value.

Example:

A company lowering prices to outcompete rivals might anticipate a price war. Instead, offering a unique product feature differentiates them without triggering retaliation.

How to Apply Game Theory in Decision-Making

1. Identify Key Players:

Consider who will be affected by your decision and how they might respond.

Example: If launching a new product, consider competitors, customers, and suppliers.

2. Map Possible Moves:

Visualize the choices available to you and others, along with their likely consequences.

Example: "If I lower prices, competitors might match me. What's my next move if that happens?"

3. Think Win-Win:

Look for strategies that benefit all parties, encouraging cooperation rather than competition.

Example: Collaborating with a competitor on industry standards might grow the market for both companies.

4. Learn from Past Patterns:

Analyze how others have behaved in similar situations to predict their next moves.

Example: "This rival tends to respond aggressively to price cuts. How can I avoid escalating the conflict?"

Everyday Example of Game Theory

You and a friend are deciding where to eat. Instead of competing over preferences, you suggest alternating choices each week, ensuring both feel satisfied in the long term.

Common Pitfalls in Game Theory

1. Overthinking Simple Decisions:

Not every situation requires complex strategic analysis.

2. Assuming Perfect Rationality:

People's emotions and biases may lead them to act unpredictably.

3. Ignoring Long-Term Relationships:

Prioritizing short-term wins over trust and collaboration can backfire.

Takeaway

Game theory teaches you to anticipate others' moves and think several steps ahead. By understanding motivations and mapping possible outcomes, you can make smarter, more strategic decisions that benefit everyone involved.

Chapter 62: The Long View

What Is the Long View?

The Long View means making decisions with a clear understanding of how they'll impact your future. It's about ensuring that today's actions align with your bigger goals, even when short-term temptations or pressures try to pull you off track.

Example:

Choosing to invest in professional development now may require sacrificing leisure time, but it pays off in long-term career growth.

Why the Long View Matters

1. Prevents Short-Sighted Decisions:

Thinking ahead helps you avoid choices that provide immediate gratification but harm your future.

2. Creates Consistency:

Long-term thinking aligns your daily actions with your larger vision.

3. Builds Resilience:

A clear focus on the future helps you weather setbacks and stay committed to your goals.

Example:

A student deciding whether to party or study before exams prioritizes studying, knowing it aligns with their goal of academic success.

How to Adopt the Long View

1. Clarify Your Goals:

Define where you want to be in the next five or ten years to guide your decisions today.

Example: "I want to become a department manager within five years, so I'll focus on leadership opportunities now."

2. Evaluate Short-Term Trade-Offs:

Consider how immediate decisions will affect your long-term progress.

Example: "Should I take this higher-paying job, or should I stick with the one that offers better growth potential?"

3. Plan Milestones:

Break your long-term goals into smaller, achievable steps to stay motivated.

Example: "If I want to run a marathon in two years, I'll start by training for a 5K within six months."

4. Regularly Reassess Your Path:

Check periodically to ensure your current actions are still aligned with your long-term vision.

Example: "Does my current spending support my goal of saving for a house?"

Everyday Example of the Long View

You're considering buying a new car. Instead of choosing the flashiest model, you opt for a reliable, fuel-efficient option that aligns with your goal of saving for retirement.

Common Pitfalls in Long-Term Thinking

1. Neglecting Present Needs:

Focusing too much on the future can leave you unprepared for immediate challenges.

2. Getting Discouraged by Slow Progress:

Long-term goals often take time, so patience is essential.

3. Failing to Adapt:

Life circumstances may change, requiring you to adjust your plans.

Takeaway

The Long View helps you align today's choices with your future goals. By staying focused on the bigger picture and balancing short-term sacrifices with long-term gains, you can build a path toward sustainable success.

Chapter 63: Scenario Thinking

What Is Scenario Thinking?

Scenario thinking involves imagining a range of possible futures and preparing for each. Rather than fixating on a single expected outcome, you explore various scenarios — good, bad, and in-between — to build flexible strategies that work across different possibilities.

Example:

A business might plan for multiple futures by considering how economic growth, stagnation, or decline could affect their operations, adjusting their strategies accordingly.

Why Scenario Thinking Matters

1. Reduces Risk:

Planning for multiple outcomes helps you prepare for unexpected challenges.

2. Improves Flexibility:

By anticipating a range of possibilities, you can adapt quickly as situations evolve.

3. Encourages Creative Problem-Solving:

Thinking beyond the "most likely" scenario opens your mind to new strategies.

Example:

A family planning a vacation considers scenarios like bad weather, budget changes, or travel delays, allowing them to create backup plans for each.

How to Practice Scenario Thinking

1. Define Your Key Question:

Start with a clear decision or goal you're trying to address.

Example: "How will my business grow in the next five years?"

2. Identify Driving Forces:

List factors that could influence your decision, such as economic trends, technological changes, or personal circumstances.

Example: "What happens if new competitors enter the market?"

3. Create Multiple Scenarios:

Develop 3–5 distinct futures: a best-case scenario, a worst-case scenario, and several plausible in-between outcomes.

Example: Best case: Revenue doubles due to market demand. Worst case: A recession cuts revenue in half.

4. Develop Action Plans:

For each scenario, outline strategies to maximize opportunities or mitigate risks.

Example: If the economy declines, the business might focus on cost-saving measures and recession-proof products.

5. Monitor and Adjust:

Continuously track key indicators to identify which scenario is unfolding and adapt your plans as needed.

Example: Rising costs might signal a need to pivot to the worst-case scenario strategy.

Everyday Example of Scenario Thinking

You're deciding whether to move to a new city for a job. Scenarios might include:

- Best case: You thrive in the role and love the city.

- Likely case: The job is good, but the city takes time to adjust to.

- Worst case: The role isn't as expected, and the move strains your finances.

By considering all outcomes, you can prepare financially and emotionally for each.

Common Pitfalls in Scenario Thinking

1. Overloading with Scenarios:

Too many scenarios can lead to confusion and indecision. Focus on 3–5 key ones.

2. Ignoring Unlikely but Impactful Scenarios:

Rare events, like economic downturns, should still be considered due to their potential impact.

3. Failing to Act:

Scenario planning is only useful if it leads to concrete strategies.

Takeaway

Scenario thinking equips you to plan for uncertainty by imagining and preparing for multiple futures. By developing flexible strategies, you can navigate unexpected challenges with confidence and resilience.

Chapter 64: Red Teaming

What Is Red Teaming?

Red Teaming is a method where you deliberately challenge your decisions or plans by adopting the role of an opponent. By thinking like critics or competitors, you identify weaknesses, test assumptions, and refine your strategies before implementing them.

Example:

A company planning a product launch might assign a "red team" to act as customers and competitors, highlighting potential flaws in the campaign.

Why Red Teaming Matters

1. Exposes Blind Spots:

By challenging assumptions, red teaming reveals weaknesses you might overlook.

2. Prepares for Countermoves:

Anticipating criticism or opposition strengthens your ability to respond effectively.

3. Improves Decision Quality:

Testing your ideas under scrutiny ensures they're robust and well-thought-out.

Example:

A non-profit uses red teaming to identify potential objections to a fundraising campaign, refining their messaging to address concerns in advance.

How to Red Team Your Decisions

1. Assemble a Red Team:

Include people who are willing to challenge ideas constructively. Ideally, choose individuals with diverse perspectives.

Example: A marketing team invites colleagues from finance and customer support to critique their strategy.

2. Set Clear Rules:

Define the scope and goals of the red team's critique to keep discussions focused.

Example: "Your role is to identify why this ad campaign might fail and propose solutions."

3. Think Like an Opponent:

Challenge every assumption, looking for vulnerabilities or overlooked risks.

Example: "What would a competitor do to outshine our product launch?"

4. Incorporate Feedback:

Use the red team's insights to strengthen your plan, address weaknesses, and develop contingency strategies.

Example: If the red team points out confusing messaging, the campaign is revised for clarity.

5. Re-Test Your Plan:

After implementing changes, run another round of critiques to ensure the strategy is solid.

Everyday Example of Red Teaming

Before buying a new home, you ask friends and family to critique your choice. One points out that the commute might be longer than expected, prompting you to reconsider.

Common Pitfalls in Red Teaming

1. Taking Criticism Personally:

Red teaming isn't about attacking you — it's about improving the plan.

2. Skipping Implementation:

Insights from red teaming are only valuable if they lead to actionable improvements.

3. Limiting Diverse Perspectives:

A homogenous red team might miss critical weaknesses.

Takeaway

Red teaming strengthens decisions by challenging them. By thinking like an opponent and refining your strategy based on critique, you can address risks, overcome blind spots, and make more robust choices.

I'm betting we'll win if we stick to our strategy.

But have you considered the odds of them countering us? Let's plan for that too.

Chapter 65: Bets and Odds

What Is Probabilistic Thinking?

Probabilistic thinking involves evaluating the likelihood of various outcomes rather than expecting certainty. It means treating decisions like bets, where you assess risks and rewards based on the odds of success. By thinking probabilistically, you reduce overconfidence and make decisions that are grounded in reality.

Example:

Before starting a business, you might estimate that you have a 60% chance of succeeding based on market research and a 40% chance of facing challenges like high competition. This helps you weigh the risks and prepare accordingly.

Why Probabilistic Thinking Matters

1. Reduces Overconfidence:

Recognizing uncertainty helps you avoid assuming your decisions are guaranteed to succeed.

2. Encourages Risk Management:

Evaluating probabilities allows you to prepare for less likely but impactful scenarios.

3. Improves Decision Accuracy:

By focusing on likelihoods, you make better-informed choices and adjust expectations.

Example:

An investor might assign probabilities to different market scenarios (growth, stagnation, decline) and diversify their portfolio to reduce risk.

How to Think Probabilistically

1. Estimate the Odds:

Assess the likelihood of various outcomes based on evidence, experience, or data.

Example: When planning a project, estimate the odds of completing it on time based on past timelines.

2. Consider the Payoffs:

Evaluate the potential benefits and losses for each outcome to determine if the risk is worth taking.

Example: If a risky investment offers a small chance of high returns and a high chance of modest losses, it may still be worth considering.

3. Prepare for Multiple Outcomes:

Develop plans for both likely and unlikely scenarios to stay adaptable.

Example: A traveler might pack for sunny weather while also including an umbrella, just in case.

4. Use Tools to Model Probabilities:

Tools like decision trees or Bayesian reasoning can help you visualize probabilities and outcomes.

Example: A decision tree might outline the probability of achieving specific sales goals under different marketing strategies.

Everyday Example of Probabilistic Thinking

You're deciding whether to buy extended insurance for a new appliance. You estimate that there's a 20% chance it will break within the warranty period. Weighing the low probability of failure against the cost of the insurance helps you decide.

Common Pitfalls in Probabilistic Thinking

1. Underestimating Rare Events:

People often dismiss unlikely scenarios, even when their impact could be significant.

2. Overvaluing Certainty:

Avoid insisting on guarantees; few decisions are risk-free.

3. Focusing Solely on Probabilities:

Probabilities are helpful, but also consider the consequences of extreme outcomes.

Takeaway

Probabilistic thinking helps you make smarter, more grounded decisions by focusing on likelihoods rather than certainties. By weighing odds, evaluating payoffs, and preparing for multiple outcomes, you can navigate uncertainty with confidence.

Chapter 66: Competitive Analysis

What Is Competitive Analysis?

Competitive analysis involves studying your rivals' strategies, strengths, and weaknesses to inform your decisions. Whether in business, sports, or personal challenges, understanding the competition allows you to anticipate moves, identify opportunities, and refine your approach.

Example:

A company researching competitors' pricing models might adjust their own pricing to offer better value or emphasize unique features.

Why Competitive Analysis Matters

1. Reveals Opportunities:

Analyzing rivals' gaps or weaknesses helps you uncover advantages.

2. Improves Strategy:

Understanding what works for competitors can inspire improvements in your own approach.

3. Prepares for Countermoves:

Anticipating rivals' actions allows you to adjust your strategy proactively.

Example:

A small bakery identifies that competitors lack gluten-free options, so they focus on offering a robust gluten-free menu to attract new customers.

How to Conduct Competitive Analysis

1. Identify Your Key Competitors:

Focus on those whose goals, audiences, or markets overlap with yours.

Example: A local coffee shop might analyze other cafes within a 5-mile radius.

2. Study Their Strengths and Weaknesses:

Look at what competitors do well and where they fall short.

Example: If a rival has great branding but slow service, you might focus on speed to stand out.

3. Analyze Their Strategy:

Study their pricing, marketing, customer base, and product offerings to understand their approach.

Example: What promotions are they running? What customer needs are they targeting?

4. Compare and Differentiate:

Use insights to highlight your unique strengths and stand out from the competition.

Example: A fitness center might focus on offering flexible class schedules if competitors prioritize high-end equipment.

5. Monitor Continuously:

Competitive landscapes evolve, so revisit your analysis regularly.

Example: Quarterly reviews of competitors' strategies help you adapt to market changes.

Everyday Example of Competitive Analysis

Before applying for a job, you review the LinkedIn profiles of other applicants to understand their skills and experiences. This helps you tailor your resume to emphasize what makes you stand out.

Common Pitfalls in Competitive Analysis

1. Copying Without Differentiation:

Mimicking competitors' strategies without highlighting your unique value leads to missed opportunities.

2. Neglecting Smaller Competitors:

Focusing only on industry leaders can cause you to underestimate emerging rivals.

3. Overanalyzing:

Spending too much time studying competitors can delay action.

Takeaway

Competitive analysis equips you with insights to anticipate moves, seize opportunities, and refine your strategies. By understanding your rivals and differentiating yourself, you can position yourself for long-term success.

Chapter 67: The Timing Factor

What Is the Timing Factor?

Timing is the art of knowing when to act. Even the best decision can fail if made too early or too late. The timing factor involves recognizing when circumstances are most favorable and striking when opportunities align.

Example:

A company launching a new product during peak holiday shopping season might achieve greater success than if they launched during a slower time of year.

Why Timing Matters

1. Maximizes Opportunities:

Acting at the right moment allows you to capitalize on favorable conditions.

2. Reduces Risks:

Waiting too long or acting prematurely can lead to missed opportunities or unnecessary risks.

3. Increases Impact:

Well-timed decisions resonate more strongly, whether in business, relationships, or personal goals.

Example:

A job seeker waits until after a company announces growth plans before applying, increasing their chances of being hired for an expanding role.

How to Master the Timing Factor

1. Study the Environment:

Observe external conditions, trends, and signals to identify the optimal moment to act.

Example: A stock trader monitors market indicators to time their investments.

2. Listen to Intuition (Backed by Evidence):

Combine gut feelings with data to sense when the moment is right.

Example: An entrepreneur might trust their intuition to pitch an idea, but only after researching the market.

3. Prepare in Advance:

Readiness allows you to act quickly when the opportunity arises.

Example: A speaker practices their presentation well in advance so they're ready when called upon.

4. Know When to Wait:

Sometimes, delaying a decision can lead to better conditions or clearer information.

Example: A homebuyer might pause their search during a seller's market to wait for prices to stabilize.

Everyday Example of Timing

Imagine you want to discuss a raise with your manager. Instead of bringing it up during a busy project, you wait until the team achieves a big success and the mood is positive.

Common Pitfalls in Timing

1. Rushing Decisions:

Acting impulsively without assessing the situation leads to poor outcomes.

2. Overanalyzing:

Waiting too long out of fear or indecision can cause you to miss the moment entirely.

3. Ignoring Trends:

Failing to recognize shifts in external factors, like market or social changes, can derail timing.

Takeaway

The timing factor is about seizing the right moment to act. By preparing, observing the environment, and balancing intuition with data, you can make impactful decisions that align perfectly with the situation.

Chapter 68: Avoiding Analysis Paralysis

What Is Analysis Paralysis?

Analysis paralysis occurs when overthinking prevents you from making a decision. You become so consumed with gathering data, weighing options, and fearing mistakes that you fail to act. While analysis is important, knowing when to stop is critical for effective decision-making.

Example:

A person researching new laptops for weeks might miss a sale or delay their purchase unnecessarily, despite already having enough information to choose.

Why Avoiding Analysis Paralysis Matters

1. Prevents Missed Opportunities:

Overthinking can cause delays that result in lost chances.

2. Saves Time and Energy:

Knowing when to stop researching frees mental resources for other priorities.

3. Reduces Stress:

Prolonged indecision can lead to frustration and burnout.

Example:

An entrepreneur debating whether to launch a product might miss the market's peak interest by overanalyzing details.

How to Avoid Analysis Paralysis

1. Set a Deadline:

Commit to a decision by a specific time to prevent endless deliberation.

Example: "I'll choose a contractor for the renovation by next Friday."

2. Prioritize Key Factors:

Focus on the most important criteria rather than getting lost in minor details.

Example: When choosing a car, prioritize reliability and cost over less critical features.

3. Limit Information Gathering:

Decide how much research is "enough" and stop once you've reached that threshold.

Example: "After reading five customer reviews, I'll make my decision."

4. Trust Your Judgment:

Recognize that no decision is ever 100% certain, and rely on your intuition when the evidence is sufficient.

Example: A couple chooses a wedding venue after narrowing it down to two strong options, trusting that both would work well.

5. Embrace Imperfection:

Accept that no decision is perfect and focus on moving forward.

Example: "Even if I make a mistake, I'll learn from it and adjust."

Everyday Example of Analysis Paralysis

You're deciding what to cook for dinner. Instead of endlessly scrolling recipes, you pick one that looks good and start cooking, saving time and stress.

Common Pitfalls in Avoiding Analysis Paralysis

1. Fear of Mistakes:

The desire for a "perfect" decision often leads to inaction.

2. Overloading with Data:

Too much information can overwhelm rather than clarify.

3. Failing to Act:

Delaying action can lead to lost opportunities or worsening situations.

Takeaway

Avoiding analysis paralysis means recognizing when you have enough information to act. By setting limits, focusing on key factors, and accepting imperfection, you can make confident decisions and avoid the trap of endless overthinking.

Chapter 69: The Power of Experimentation

What Is Experimentation in Decision-Making?

Experimentation involves testing ideas or options on a small scale before fully committing to them. It's a practical way to gather real-world feedback, validate assumptions, and refine your approach. Instead of making decisions based solely on predictions, you use experiments to confirm what works.

Example:

A company testing a new product might release it to a small market segment first, learning from customer feedback before launching on a larger scale.

Why Experimentation Matters

1. Reduces Risk:

Testing ideas on a small scale allows you to identify issues and make adjustments before committing significant resources.

2. Provides Data-Driven Insights:

Experiments yield concrete evidence about what works and what doesn't.

3. Encourages Innovation:

Experimentation fosters a mindset of curiosity and learning, helping you explore unconventional solutions.

Example:

A writer considering self-publishing tests the waters by releasing a short story online to gauge interest and refine their marketing approach.

How to Use Experimentation in Decision-Making

1. Define Your Hypothesis:

Clearly state what you want to test and what outcome you expect.

Example: "If I market the product to younger audiences, I expect higher engagement rates."

2. Start Small:

Test your idea with minimal resources or on a small scale to limit risk.

Example: Launch a beta version of your app with a small user group before a full release.

3. Measure Results:

Collect data to evaluate the success of your experiment against your goals.

Example: Track conversion rates during a trial marketing campaign to determine its effectiveness.

4. Refine and Retest:

Use the insights gained to improve your approach and test again if necessary.

Example: Adjust an ad's messaging based on feedback and run a second test to see if it performs better.

5. Scale Up:

Once your experiment proves successful, expand your efforts with confidence.

Example: A café introduces a new menu item after a successful trial with regular customers.

Everyday Example of Experimentation

You're considering switching careers but aren't sure if the new field is right for you. You take a short online course or freelance part-time to test your interest and aptitude before fully committing.

Common Pitfalls in Experimentation

1. Skipping the Testing Phase:

Jumping straight into full-scale decisions can lead to costly mistakes.

2. Overcomplicating Experiments:

Simple tests are often more effective than elaborate ones.

3. Ignoring Results:

Experiments are only valuable if you use the insights to refine your approach.

Takeaway

Experimentation turns uncertainty into opportunity by testing your ideas in real-world conditions. By starting small, measuring results, and refining your approach, you can make informed decisions with confidence.

Chapter 70: Strategic Patience

What Is Strategic Patience?

Strategic patience is the ability to delay action until conditions are optimal. It's not about passivity or procrastination but about knowing when to wait and when to act. Timing is everything, and sometimes, waiting for the right moment can make the difference between failure and success.

Example:

An investor who waits for the market to stabilize before buying stocks demonstrates strategic patience, maximizing returns while minimizing risk.

Why Strategic Patience Matters

1. Improves Decision Quality:

Rushing into decisions can lead to mistakes. Waiting provides clarity and better conditions for action.

2. Maximizes Resources:

Acting too soon can waste time, energy, or money. Patience ensures you use resources effectively.

3. Builds Long-Term Success:

Delayed gratification often leads to more substantial rewards than short-term gains.

Example:

An entrepreneur waits for technology costs to drop before launching a product, ensuring it's more affordable to produce and sell.

How to Cultivate Strategic Patience

1. Recognize the Value of Timing:

Assess whether the current conditions are favorable for action or if waiting would yield better results.

Example: A professional postpones a major career move until after completing a key certification.

2. Monitor Key Indicators:

Keep track of trends, signals, or events that might influence the right moment to act.

Example: A business monitors consumer demand before launching a new product line.

3. Stay Focused on Your Goals:

Patience is easier when you have a clear vision of what you're working toward.

Example: A family delays purchasing a home until they save enough for a larger down payment, reducing financial strain.

4. Prepare While You Wait:

Use the waiting period to refine your plans, gather resources, or build skills.

Example: While waiting for the market to improve, an investor studies new strategies to maximize future returns.

5. Know When to Stop Waiting:

Patience should not become inaction. Identify deadlines or conditions that signal when it's time to act.

Example: A startup sets a launch deadline to ensure they don't wait so long that competitors gain an advantage.

Everyday Example of Strategic Patience

You're considering buying a car but notice that dealerships often run sales at the end of the year. By waiting, you can purchase the same car at a lower price.

Common Pitfalls in Strategic Patience

1. Confusing Patience with Procrastination:

Waiting must be intentional and strategic, not an excuse to avoid decisions.

2. Missing Opportunities:

Waiting too long can cause you to lose out on favorable conditions.

3. Losing Focus:

Over time, distractions can derail your goals if you're not actively preparing.

Takeaway

Strategic patience is a powerful decision-making tool when used wisely. By recognizing the value of timing, preparing while you wait, and knowing when to act, you can seize opportunities at their peak and achieve greater success.

Part VIII: Everyday Decision-Making

Big life decisions often come down to practical choices. From career paths to financial goals, daily decisions shape the trajectory of your life. This section provides actionable strategies to navigate common yet critical decisions with clarity, confidence, and balance.

Chapter 71: Choosing Careers

What Does It Mean to Align Passion and Practicality?

Choosing a career involves balancing what excites you (passion) with what sustains you financially and practically (practicality). While passion gives you purpose and motivation, practicality ensures long-term stability and growth. The best career decisions blend these elements to create a fulfilling and sustainable path.

Example:

A person passionate about teaching but concerned about income stability might choose to tutor online part-time while pursuing a teaching credential.

Why Aligning Passion and Practicality Matters

1. Sustains Long-Term Motivation:

A career driven by passion is more likely to keep you engaged and energized.

2. Ensures Financial Stability:

Practicality helps you make choices that support your financial goals and responsibilities.

3. Promotes Personal Fulfillment:

Combining both leads to a sense of purpose and balance in your work life.

Example:

An artist passionate about painting may pursue a graphic design job for financial stability while building their painting portfolio on the side.

How to Choose a Career with Balance

1. Assess Your Interests and Skills:

Reflect on what you enjoy and where your strengths lie.

Example: "I love problem-solving and excel at communication. What careers align with these traits?"

2. Evaluate Market Demand:

Research industries or roles that match your interests and are in demand.

Example: A person interested in technology might explore roles like software development or data analysis, which have strong job prospects.

3. Set Financial and Lifestyle Goals:

Determine what income and work-life balance you need to feel secure and satisfied.

Example: If travel is important to you, a remote or flexible job might be a priority.

4. Start Small, Then Build:

Explore your passion through side projects or part-time work before fully committing.

Example: A baking enthusiast starts by selling goods at farmers' markets before opening a bakery.

5. Be Open to Evolution:

Your passions and circumstances may change over time. Stay flexible and adjust your path as needed.

Example: A journalist transitions to content marketing to pursue better pay while still leveraging their writing skills.

Everyday Example of Career Alignment

Someone passionate about fitness might start as a personal trainer but later transition to opening their own gym, combining their love for exercise with entrepreneurial goals.

Common Pitfalls in Career Decisions

1. Choosing Passion Alone:

Ignoring financial realities can lead to burnout or instability.

2. Prioritizing Practicality Too Much:

Overemphasizing stability can leave you feeling unfulfilled.

3. Fearing Change:

Sticking to a career out of comfort or habit may prevent growth.

Takeaway

The best career decisions balance passion and practicality. By aligning what you love with what sustains you, you can build a career that's both fulfilling and realistic.

Chapter 72: Financial Decisions

What Does It Mean to Invest in What Matters?

Financial decisions aren't just about saving or spending; they're about aligning your resources with your values, priorities, and long-term goals. Investing in what matters ensures your money supports both your immediate needs and your future ambitions.

Example:

Instead of buying an expensive car to impress others, a person might prioritize saving for a home, which aligns with their long-term goal of stability.

Why Smart Financial Decisions Matter

1. Builds Stability:

Prioritizing needs over impulsive wants creates a strong financial foundation.

2. Achieves Long-Term Goals:

Investing in what matters helps you stay on track with life objectives like education, retirement, or family needs.

3. Reduces Stress:

Financial security minimizes anxiety about unexpected expenses or future uncertainties.

Example:

A family sets aside a portion of their income for an emergency fund before planning a vacation, ensuring they're prepared for unplanned costs.

How to Make Financial Decisions Wisely

1. Clarify Your Priorities:

Identify your short- and long-term goals, like paying off debt, saving for retirement, or funding a passion project.

Example: "I want to save $10,000 for a down payment on a house within three years."

2. Separate Needs from Wants:

Focus on essentials first, then allocate resources to discretionary spending.

Example: Pay your bills and build savings before splurging on a luxury item.

3. Create a Budget:

Plan your spending and saving to ensure you stay within your means.

Example: Use the 50/30/20 rule: 50% for needs, 30% for wants, and 20% for savings or debt repayment.

4. Evaluate Opportunities for Growth:

Invest in education, skills, or assets that increase your earning potential.

Example: Take a certification course that boosts your qualifications for a higher-paying job.

5. Think Ahead:

Regularly review your financial plans to adjust for life changes or new goals.

Example: After starting a family, you might prioritize saving for your children's education.

Everyday Example of Investing in What Matters

You're deciding between upgrading to the latest phone or starting an emergency savings fund. By choosing savings, you're investing in long-term security over short-term gratification.

Common Pitfalls in Financial Decisions

1. Living Beyond Your Means:

Overspending on wants can leave you unprepared for future expenses.

2. Failing to Save Early:

Delaying savings, especially for retirement, reduces long-term benefits.

3. Neglecting Investments in Growth:

Focusing solely on immediate needs may hinder opportunities for advancement.

Takeaway

Smart financial decisions are about prioritizing what truly matters. By aligning your spending and savings with your goals, you can build a secure future while enjoying life's rewards.

Chapter 73: Time Management

What Is Time Management?

Time management is the deliberate planning and control of how you spend your hours to maximize productivity and achieve your goals. It's about aligning your daily actions with what truly matters, avoiding wasted effort, and maintaining balance between work, rest, and personal priorities.

Example:

A busy parent prioritizes tasks by using the early morning for focused work, reserving the evening for family time, and limiting distractions during key hours.

Why Time Management Matters

1. Increases Productivity:

Structuring your day allows you to accomplish more in less time.

2. Reduces Stress:

Knowing you've allocated time for critical tasks helps you feel in control.

3. Achieves Work-Life Balance:

Time management ensures you dedicate hours to both professional and personal priorities.

Example:

A freelancer uses time-blocking to assign specific hours for client work, exercise, and relaxation, preventing burnout.

How to Manage Time Effectively

1. Set Priorities:

Identify the most important tasks each day and focus on completing them first.

Example: Use the Eisenhower Matrix to distinguish between urgent and important tasks.

2. Use Time-Blocking:

Schedule specific blocks of time for key activities to minimize multitasking.

Example: Reserve 9–11 AM for deep work and 2–3 PM for emails and meetings.

3. Limit Distractions:

Remove interruptions like phone notifications or unnecessary meetings during focus periods.

Example: Turn off social media alerts while working on a project.

4. Plan Tomorrow, Today:

At the end of each day, review what you've accomplished and prepare your task list for tomorrow.

Example: Write down the top three tasks to tackle first thing in the morning.

5. Schedule Breaks:

Taking regular breaks improves focus and prevents burnout.

Example: Use the Pomodoro Technique: work for 25 minutes, then take a 5-minute break.

Everyday Example of Time Management

A student juggling school and part-time work schedules their day: mornings for classes, afternoons for work, and evenings for studying. Allocating specific time slots helps them avoid last-minute cramming or missed deadlines.

Common Pitfalls in Time Management

1. Overloading Your Schedule:

Packing too much into one day leads to overwhelm and decreased productivity.

2. Procrastinating on Key Tasks:

Delaying important work wastes valuable time and creates unnecessary stress.

3. Failing to Adjust Plans:

Sticking rigidly to a plan without adapting to new priorities can backfire.

Takeaway

Effective time management is the foundation for accomplishing your goals and maintaining balance. By setting priorities, reducing distractions, and planning ahead, you can make every hour count and live a more focused, productive life.

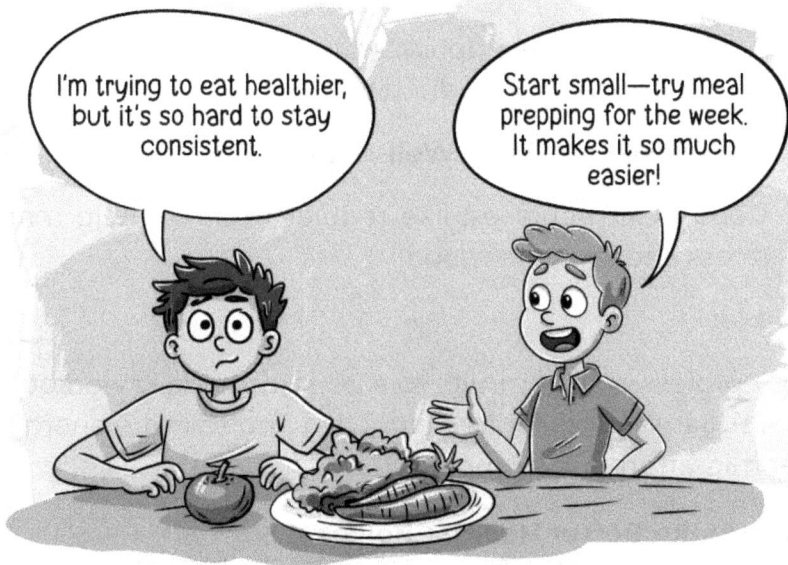

I'm trying to eat healthier, but it's so hard to stay consistent.

Start small—try meal prepping for the week. It makes it so much easier!

Chapter 74: Health Choices

What Are Health Choices?

Health choices are the daily decisions that influence your physical, mental, and emotional well-being. Whether it's what you eat, how you exercise, or how much sleep you get, these decisions build the foundation for a longer, healthier life.

Example:

Choosing to walk to work instead of driving not only supports physical fitness but also reduces stress and boosts mental clarity.

Why Health Choices Matter

1. Prevents Chronic Illness:

Healthy habits reduce the risk of conditions like heart disease, diabetes, and obesity.

2. Boosts Energy and Focus:

A healthy lifestyle improves physical stamina and mental clarity, enhancing productivity.

3. Enhances Emotional Well-Being:

Good health choices, like regular exercise, help manage stress and improve mood.

Example:

A busy professional commits to a 20-minute daily workout and swaps sugary snacks for fresh fruit, leading to more energy and fewer mid-afternoon slumps.

How to Make Better Health Choices

1. Start Small:

Focus on simple, manageable changes rather than trying to overhaul everything at once.

Example: Begin by drinking an extra glass of water daily or walking 10 minutes a day.

2. Prioritize Consistency Over Perfection:

Build habits that you can sustain, even if progress is gradual.

Example: If you can't do a full workout, opt for stretching or light activity instead.

3. Plan Your Meals:

Prepare healthy meals in advance to avoid impulsive, unhealthy eating.

Example: Cook several portions of lean protein and vegetables on Sunday for easy weekday lunches.

4. Schedule Sleep:

Treat sleep as a non-negotiable priority for recovery and mental clarity.

Example: Set a regular bedtime and avoid screens an hour before bed.

5. Listen to Your Body:

Pay attention to how your choices affect your energy, mood, and physical health.

Example: Notice if certain foods make you feel sluggish and adjust your diet accordingly.

Everyday Example of Health Choices

Instead of skipping breakfast, you prepare a quick smoothie with fruits and protein. This simple decision sets the tone for a more energetic and productive day.

Common Pitfalls in Health Decisions

1. Focusing on Short-Term Fixes:

Crash diets or extreme exercise routines are rarely sustainable.

2. Neglecting Mental Health:

Physical health is vital, but mental well-being is equally important.

3. All-or-Nothing Thinking:

Skipping one workout doesn't mean you should abandon your fitness plan entirely.

Takeaway

Your health choices shape every aspect of your life. By focusing on small, consistent actions that support your physical and mental well-being, you can create a healthier, more balanced lifestyle.

Chapter 75: Relationship Decisions

What Are Relationship Decisions?

Relationship decisions involve navigating choices in your personal and professional connections, from forming friendships to handling conflicts or ending toxic dynamics. These decisions often require balancing emotional impulses with logical thinking to maintain healthy, meaningful bonds.

Example:

Choosing to calmly address a disagreement with a friend rather than reacting emotionally preserves trust and mutual respect.

Why Balancing Logic and Emotion Matters

1. Promotes Healthy Communication:

Logical thinking prevents emotional outbursts, while empathy fosters understanding.

2. Strengthens Connections:

Decisions rooted in mutual respect and clear reasoning build stronger relationships.

3. Reduces Regret:

Balancing emotion with rationality helps you avoid impulsive choices that might harm the relationship.

Example in Action:

A manager giving constructive feedback uses empathy to consider the employee's feelings while logically focusing on performance improvement.

How to Balance Logic and Emotion in Relationships

1. Pause Before Reacting:

Give yourself time to process emotions before responding to conflicts or challenges.

Example: Take a few deep breaths before replying to a heated text message.

2. Identify Core Values:

Use your personal principles as a guide to make decisions aligned with what matters most.

Example: If honesty is a key value, prioritize open communication even during tough conversations.

3. Practice Active Listening:

Empathize with the other person's perspective to ensure your decisions consider their feelings.

Example: Paraphrase their concerns to confirm understanding: "It sounds like you're worried about..."

4. Separate Emotion from Fact:

Acknowledge your feelings, but focus on the facts to determine the best course of action.

Example: In a disagreement with a partner, identify the actual issue rather than letting frustration guide your response.

5. Use "I" Statements:

Frame your concerns without blaming the other person to encourage productive dialogue.

Example: "I feel overwhelmed when the chores pile up; can we create a plan together?"

Everyday Example of Relationship Decisions

You're upset with a co-worker who missed a deadline. Instead of lashing out, you calmly work together to prevent it from happening again.

Common Pitfalls in Relationship Decisions

1. Reacting Emotionally:

Acting on anger or frustration can damage trust and escalate conflicts.

2. Overthinking:

Overanalyzing every interaction can lead to unnecessary tension or indecision.

3. Ignoring Red Flags:

Dismissing signs of toxic behavior to preserve a relationship often leads to long-term harm.

Takeaway

Balancing logic and emotion helps you navigate relationship decisions with clarity and empathy. By pausing to reflect, communicating thoughtfully, and focusing on shared values, you can strengthen connections while making healthier choices for yourself and others.

Chapter 76: Parenting with Purpose

What Does Parenting with Purpose Mean?

Parenting with purpose means making decisions that reflect your family's values and priorities. It's about guiding your children with intention, balancing discipline and support, and fostering a healthy environment where they can thrive.

Example:

Choosing to limit screen time and encourage outdoor activities aligns with a value of promoting physical and mental health.

Why Intentional Parenting Matters

1. Builds Stronger Bonds:

Purposeful decisions foster trust and open communication within the family.

2. Shapes Children's Growth:

Consistent, intentional choices provide a stable foundation for emotional and intellectual development.

3. Reduces Stress:

A clear parenting approach minimizes confusion and conflict in day-to-day family life.

Example:

A parent sets a bedtime routine that includes reading together, promoting both connection and good sleep habits.

How to Parent with Purpose

1. Define Family Values:

Decide what principles are most important to your family, such as kindness, education, or independence.

Example: "Our family prioritizes honesty, so we'll model and reward open communication."

2. Set Consistent Boundaries:

Clear rules provide structure and help children understand expectations.

Example: "Homework comes before screen time, every day."

3. Foster Open Dialogue:

Encourage children to express their thoughts and feelings to build trust and understanding.

Example: "How did that situation make you feel? Let's talk about what we can learn from it."

4. Adapt as They Grow:

Parenting decisions should evolve to reflect your children's changing needs and abilities.

Example: As a teenager gains independence, involve them in decisions about curfews or responsibilities.

5. Model the Behavior You Want to See:

Children learn more from what you do than what you say.

Example: Demonstrate patience and empathy when resolving family conflicts.

Everyday Example of Parenting with Purpose

When a child struggles with a school subject, the parent prioritizes encouragement over criticism, seeking solutions like tutoring or extra practice to build confidence and skills.

Common Pitfalls in Parenting Decisions

1. Inconsistency:

Changing rules or expectations confuses children and undermines trust.

2. Overcontrolling:

Micromanaging stifles independence and decision-making skills.

3. Ignoring Self-Care:

Neglecting your well-being makes it harder to parent effectively.

Takeaway

Parenting with purpose ensures your decisions align with your family's values and long-term goals. By fostering connection, setting consistent boundaries, and adapting to your child's needs, you can create a nurturing environment that supports their growth.

Chapter 77: Buying Smart

What Does It Mean to Buy Smart?

Buying smart means making thoughtful, informed decisions about big purchases to ensure they align with your financial goals, values, and long-term needs. It's about balancing quality, cost, and purpose to get the most value for your money without unnecessary regret.

Example:

Instead of impulsively buying the latest tech gadget, a person researches options, compares prices, and waits for a sale to make a smart purchase.

Why Buying Smart Matters

1. Protects Your Financial Health:

Overspending on big purchases can strain your budget or lead to debt.

2. Ensures Long-Term Satisfaction:

Smart purchases are more likely to meet your needs and provide value over time.

3. Reduces Buyer's Remorse:

Thoughtful decision-making prevents regret over unnecessary or poorly chosen purchases.

Example:

A family choosing a home considers location, school quality, and resale value to ensure the purchase fits their current and future needs.

How to Evaluate Big Purchases Wisely

1. Define Your Needs and Priorities:

List the essential features or criteria the purchase must meet.

Example: When buying a car, prioritize fuel efficiency, reliability, and maintenance costs.

2. Set a Budget:

Determine what you can afford, including hidden costs like taxes, maintenance, or upgrades.

Example: A homebuyer accounts for property taxes and closing costs when setting their maximum budget.

3. Research Thoroughly:

Compare options, read reviews, and ask for recommendations to ensure you make an informed choice.

Example: A shopper considering a TV compares models, checks warranties, and waits for a holiday sale.

4. Delay Impulse Purchases:

Give yourself time to reflect before committing to significant expenses.

Example: Use a 30-day rule: wait a month before making a major purchase to ensure it's necessary.

5. Think Long-Term:

Consider how the purchase will hold up over time and align with your future needs.

Example: A young professional invests in a high-quality laptop knowing it will last several years.

Everyday Example of Smart Buying

You're upgrading your smartphone. Instead of buying the most expensive model, you compare features, trade-in values, and promotions, choosing the option that balances price and functionality.

Common Pitfalls in Big Purchases

1. Focusing on Trends:

Buying based on hype often leads to regret when trends fade or the item doesn't meet your needs.

2. Overlooking Hidden Costs:

Failing to account for ongoing expenses like maintenance or energy usage can strain your budget.

3. Skipping Research:

Rushing into a purchase without comparing options can result in lower quality or higher costs.

Takeaway

Smart buying ensures that your big purchases align with your financial goals and provide long-term value. By focusing on needs, setting a budget, and researching options, you can make confident, regret-free decisions.

Chapter 78: Where to Live

What Does It Mean to Assess Location Choices Effectively?

Choosing where to live is one of life's biggest decisions, affecting your career, relationships, finances, and quality of life. Assessing location choices effectively means weighing factors like cost, opportunities, and lifestyle to ensure your new home aligns with your needs and goals.

Example:

A person moving for work compares neighborhoods based on commute times, affordability, and access to amenities like parks and schools.

Why Location Decisions Matter

1. Impacts Finances:

Housing costs, taxes, and living expenses vary widely by location.

2. Shapes Lifestyle:

Where you live influences your access to work, recreation, and social connections.

3. Affects Long-Term Plans:

Your location may determine your career opportunities, children's education, or ability to save for the future.

Example:

A couple deciding between urban and suburban living considers their priorities: proximity to work vs. access to larger living spaces and good schools.

How to Evaluate Where to Live

1. Identify Key Priorities:

Rank factors like affordability, commute, safety, climate, and community based on your needs.

Example: A remote worker prioritizes affordability and outdoor activities over proximity to an office.

2. Research Costs of Living:

Compare housing, utilities, groceries, and taxes in potential locations to ensure affordability.

Example: A person moving to a new city calculates their budget based on local rent and transportation costs.

3. Consider Career Opportunities:

Ensure the location supports your professional goals, whether through job availability or networking opportunities.

Example: A tech professional might prioritize living in a city with a thriving tech industry.

4. Visit Before Committing:

Spend time in the area to get a sense of its vibe, amenities, and suitability for your lifestyle.

Example: Before relocating, a family explores potential neighborhoods, visiting schools and parks.

5. Plan for the Long Term:

Evaluate how the location fits your future plans, such as raising children or retiring.

Example: A young couple buys a starter home in an area with good schools, anticipating their family's growth.

Everyday Example of Location Decisions

You're offered a job in another city. Before moving, you research neighborhoods, commute options, and social activities to ensure it's a good fit for your career and lifestyle.

Common Pitfalls in Location Decisions

1. Focusing Only on the Job:

Moving solely for work can backfire if the location doesn't align with your personal needs.

2. Underestimating Costs:

Ignoring expenses like taxes, insurance, or transportation can strain your finances.

3. Neglecting Lifestyle Preferences:

Choosing a location that doesn't suit your hobbies, values, or social preferences can lead to dissatisfaction.

Takeaway

Choosing where to live is about aligning location factors with your goals and values. By prioritizing your needs, researching thoroughly, and considering long-term plans, you can make a decision that enhances both your lifestyle and future.

Chapter 79: Handling Crises

What Does It Mean to Handle Crises Effectively?

Crisis decision-making involves navigating high-pressure situations where time, resources, and emotions are limited. It's about staying calm, prioritizing effectively, and taking decisive action, even in the face of uncertainty or risk.

Example:

During a sudden financial setback, a family decides to pause discretionary spending, create a revised budget, and prioritize essential expenses like rent and groceries.

Why Effective Crisis Management Matters

1. Minimizes Harm:

Quick, well-thought-out actions reduce negative consequences during emergencies.

2. Restores Stability:

Decisive responses help you regain control and prevent the crisis from worsening.

3. Builds Confidence:

Successfully managing a crisis strengthens your ability to handle future challenges.

Example:

A business experiencing a supply chain disruption develops a backup supplier relationship, ensuring minimal delays in product delivery.

How to Make Decisions Under Pressure

1. Pause and Assess:

Take a moment to understand the situation before acting impulsively.

Example: Ask, "What's the immediate problem, and what resources do I have to address it?"

2. Prioritize Urgent Actions:

Focus on immediate steps to address the most critical aspects of the crisis.

Example: During a power outage, prioritize securing food and medical supplies before addressing long-term solutions.

3. Delegate When Possible:

Share responsibilities to lighten the load and ensure faster action.

Example: In a workplace emergency, assign tasks to team members based on their strengths.

4. Communicate Clearly:

Keep stakeholders informed to avoid misunderstandings and foster collaboration.

Example: In a family crisis, share updates and plans to ensure everyone is on the same page.

5. Learn from the Experience:

After the crisis, review what worked, what didn't, and how to improve for the future.

Example: A company analyzes how they handled a PR crisis to create a stronger response plan for similar situations.

Everyday Example of Crisis Decision-Making

During a sudden illness, you reschedule non-urgent appointments, focus on rest and recovery, and ask a friend for help with daily errands to manage the situation effectively.

Common Pitfalls in Crisis Decisions

1. Panicking:

Acting out of fear or anxiety can lead to rash, ineffective choices.

2. Overthinking:

Delaying action to analyze every detail wastes precious time in emergencies.

3. Neglecting Communication:

Failing to involve others can result in confusion and missed opportunities for support.

Takeaway

Handling crises effectively means staying calm, prioritizing key actions, and maintaining clear communication. By breaking the situation into manageable steps and learning from the experience, you can turn high-pressure moments into opportunities for growth and resilience.

Chapter 80: The Minimalist Mindset

What Is the Minimalist Mindset?

The minimalist mindset focuses on reducing unnecessary choices and distractions, allowing you to concentrate on what truly matters. Simplifying decision-making eliminates overwhelm and conserves mental energy for the most important tasks.

Example:

A busy professional simplifies their wardrobe to a few versatile outfits, saving time and energy each morning.

Why a Minimalist Mindset Matters

1. Reduces Decision Fatigue:

Simplifying choices conserves mental resources for more critical decisions.

2. Improves Focus:

Eliminating distractions helps you concentrate on your priorities.

3. Enhances Clarity:

Simplified decision-making reduces stress and boosts confidence in your choices.

Example:

A couple planning a wedding limits their options for venues and vendors, focusing on those that align with their budget and style, reducing stress and simplifying the process.

How to Adopt a Minimalist Mindset

1. Identify Priorities:

Focus on the choices that truly align with your goals and values.

Example: When shopping, prioritize quality over quantity to avoid clutter.

2. Limit Options:

Set boundaries for how many options you'll consider to avoid overwhelm.

Example: Narrow your restaurant choices to three options instead of scrolling endlessly.

3. Create Systems:

Establish routines and defaults to reduce everyday decision-making.

Example: Meal prep once a week to avoid daily decisions about what to cook.

4. Declutter Your Environment:

A clean, organized space supports clearer thinking and faster decisions.

Example: Clear your desk of unnecessary items to focus better on work.

5. Embrace "Good Enough":

Avoid perfectionism by choosing what works well instead of waiting for the ideal option.

Example: Pick a gym that's convenient rather than searching endlessly for the "perfect" facility.

Everyday Example of the Minimalist Mindset

You're planning a vacation. Instead of overwhelming yourself with dozens of destinations, you focus on three locations that meet your top priorities: affordability, activities, and weather.

Common Pitfalls in Simplifying Decisions

1. Over-Simplifying Important Choices:

Reducing options too much can overlook crucial factors in complex decisions.

2. Avoiding Exploration:

Always choosing the same thing can lead to missed opportunities for growth or discovery.

3. Focusing Only on Efficiency:

A minimalist approach should balance simplicity with meaningful outcomes.

Takeaway

A minimalist mindset simplifies decision-making by reducing distractions and focusing on essentials. By narrowing options, creating systems, and prioritizing what matters most, you free your mind to make thoughtful, impactful choices.

Part IX: Advanced Decision-Making

As decisions become more complex, so does the need for advanced tools. This section focuses on strategies to refine your decision-making process, manage mental load, and navigate high-stakes situations. These advanced techniques help you think critically, act decisively, and continually improve.

Chapter 81: Cognitive Load Management

What Is Cognitive Load Management?

Cognitive load management involves reducing the mental strain caused by too much information or too many decisions. It's about organizing your thoughts, prioritizing tasks, and simplifying processes to free up mental resources for more important decisions.

Example:

A manager facing multiple deadlines delegates routine tasks to their team, allowing them to focus on strategic planning.

Why Cognitive Load Management Matters

1. Improves Focus:

A clear mind processes information more effectively and avoids distractions.

2. Reduces Decision Fatigue:

Limiting mental strain prevents burnout and improves the quality of your choices.

3. Boosts Creativity:

Freeing up mental space encourages innovative thinking and problem-solving.

Example:

A busy professional organizes their day with time-blocking, reserving the morning for deep work and the afternoon for meetings, avoiding cognitive overload.

How to Manage Cognitive Load

1. Prioritize Tasks:

Focus on the most critical and time-sensitive activities to avoid being overwhelmed.

Example: Use a task management system like "Must-Do, Should-Do, Nice-to-Do" to organize your day.

2. Limit Multitasking:

Concentrate on one task at a time to improve efficiency and reduce errors.

Example: Silence notifications while writing a report to maintain focus.

3. Declutter Your Mind:

Write down thoughts, tasks, or ideas to free up mental bandwidth.

Example: Use a notebook or app to create a running to-do list, so you don't rely on memory alone.

4. Automate Routine Decisions:

Create habits or defaults for recurring choices to conserve mental energy.

Example: Plan weekly meals in advance to avoid daily dinner decisions.

5. Take Breaks:

Regular breaks recharge your mind and improve decision-making capacity.

Example: Step away from work for a 10-minute walk after completing a major task.

Everyday Example of Cognitive Load Management

You're overwhelmed by a cluttered inbox. Instead of sorting everything manually, you create filters for newsletters, prioritize urgent emails, and unsubscribe from unnecessary ones, making it easier to focus.

Common Pitfalls in Cognitive Load Management

1. Ignoring Limits:

Taking on too much leads to mistakes and burnout.

2. Overcomplicating Systems:

Overly complex organizational methods can become a source of stress.

3. Neglecting Rest:

Failing to recharge your mind reduces your ability to make sound decisions.

Takeaway

Cognitive load management keeps your mind sharp by reducing unnecessary mental strain. By prioritizing tasks, automating routines, and taking breaks, you create the mental clarity needed for high-quality decision-making.

Chapter 82: Learning from Failure

What Does It Mean to Learn from Failure?

Learning from failure means analyzing mistakes to identify valuable insights and apply those lessons to future decisions. It shifts the focus from regret to growth, turning setbacks into opportunities for improvement.

Example:

After a failed project launch, a team identifies poor market research as the cause and commits to more thorough data collection for future initiatives.

Why Learning from Failure Matters

1. Builds Resilience:

Viewing failure as part of the learning process reduces fear and promotes persistence.

2. Improves Future Decisions:

Analyzing mistakes helps you avoid repeating them and refine your strategies.

3. Encourages Innovation:

Taking risks often leads to breakthroughs, even if some attempts fail.

Example:

A student learns from failing an exam by identifying their weak study habits and adopting new methods, leading to better performance next time.

How to Learn from Failure

1. Acknowledge the Failure:

Accept what went wrong without deflecting blame or ignoring the issue.

Example: "I didn't meet my deadline because I underestimated the time needed for research."

2. Analyze the Causes:

Break down the factors that led to failure to identify patterns or areas for improvement.

Example: "I spent too much time on minor details instead of focusing on the big picture."

3. Focus on Lessons, Not Regrets:

Use the experience to uncover actionable insights rather than dwelling on the setback.

Example: "Next time, I'll create a more realistic timeline with clear milestones."

4. Apply What You've Learned:

Implement changes based on your analysis to improve future outcomes.

Example: A small business owner refines their marketing strategy after noticing low engagement with previous campaigns.

5. Celebrate Resilience:

Recognize the effort you put into bouncing back to stay motivated.

Example: "Even though the pitch failed, I learned how to refine my presentation skills for next time."

Everyday Example of Learning from Failure

You burn dinner while trying a new recipe. Instead of giving up on cooking, you identify where you went wrong — like misreading the instructions — and approach the next attempt more carefully.

Common Pitfalls in Learning from Failure

1. Ignoring the Lesson:

Failing without reflection ensures the same mistakes will happen again.

2. Focusing on Blame:

Assigning fault to others rather than assessing your own role limits growth.

3. Avoiding Risk:

Fear of failure can prevent you from taking valuable opportunities.

Takeaway

Failure isn't the end — it's a stepping stone to better decisions. By analyzing mistakes, focusing on lessons, and applying new strategies, you can turn setbacks into powerful tools for growth and resilience.

Chapter 83: Bias Audits

What Is a Bias Audit?

A bias audit involves regularly reviewing your decisions and thought processes to identify and correct cognitive biases. These mental shortcuts can distort your judgment, leading to flawed conclusions. By auditing your biases, you enhance your ability to think critically and make rational choices.

Example:

Before hiring a candidate, a manager reviews their notes to ensure they're not favoring someone based on shared interests instead of qualifications.

Why Bias Audits Matter

1. Improves Decision Accuracy:

Recognizing biases ensures your decisions are based on facts, not distorted perceptions.

2. Encourages Objectivity:

Auditing helps you stay neutral, especially in emotionally charged situations.

3. Promotes Fairness:

Reducing biases leads to more equitable outcomes, whether in personal relationships or professional settings.

Example:

A teacher evaluating students' work checks for bias by grading assignments without knowing who submitted them.

How to Conduct a Bias Audit

1. Identify Common Biases:

Familiarize yourself with cognitive biases like confirmation bias (favoring evidence that supports your beliefs) or loss aversion (fearing losses more than valuing gains).

Example: Recognize that you might be anchoring on the first piece of information you received about a decision.

2. Review Past Decisions:

Reflect on key decisions to identify patterns where biases may have influenced your judgment.

Example: "Did I overvalue advice from someone just because they seemed confident?"

3. Challenge Assumptions:

Question the reasoning behind your choices to uncover hidden biases.

Example: "Am I favoring this idea because it aligns with what I already believe?"

4. Seek Diverse Perspectives:

Invite input from others to challenge your thinking and expose blind spots.

Example: "What do you see in this situation that I might be missing?"

5. Create a Bias Checklist:

Use a checklist to remind yourself of potential biases during key decisions.

Example: Before making a choice, ask, "Am I relying on stereotypes or overlooking contradictory evidence?"

Everyday Example of a Bias Audit

When planning a vacation, you notice you're favoring a destination based on flashy marketing rather than researching practical details like cost and activities. By auditing your choice, you adjust your decision to better suit your needs.

Common Pitfalls in Bias Audits

1. Assuming You're Unbiased:

Everyone has biases, and failing to acknowledge them hinders growth.

2. Overlooking Emotional Factors:

Ignoring how emotions influence decisions can lead to incomplete audits.

3. Relying on Self-Reflection Alone:

Without external feedback, it's easy to miss hidden biases.

Takeaway

Bias audits are essential for clear, objective decision-making. By identifying and challenging cognitive biases, you ensure your choices are rational, fair, and aligned with reality.

Chapter 84: The Power of Small Wins

What Are Small Wins?

Small wins are minor but meaningful accomplishments that build confidence, motivation, and momentum toward larger goals. They create a positive feedback loop, turning incremental progress into long-term success.

Example:

A student struggling with a large project starts by completing one section at a time, gaining momentum with each small victory.

Why Small Wins Matter

1. Boost Confidence:

Achieving small goals reinforces your belief in your abilities.

2. Sustain Motivation:

Regular progress keeps you engaged and focused on your larger objectives.

3. Reduce Overwhelm:

Breaking big tasks into smaller steps makes them more manageable.

Example:

A person saving for a house celebrates reaching each $1,000 milestone, motivating them to stay on track.

How to Leverage Small Wins

1. Set Micro-Goals:

Break big goals into smaller, achievable steps.

Example: Instead of "Write a book," start with "Draft the first chapter."

2. Track Progress:

Record each accomplishment to visualize your growth.

Example: Use a habit tracker to log daily workouts as part of a fitness goal.

3. Celebrate Success:

Acknowledge even minor achievements to stay motivated.

Example: Reward yourself with a small treat after completing a challenging task.

4. Focus on Consistency:

Regular small wins are more impactful than occasional big ones.

Example: Write 300 words daily instead of waiting for inspiration to finish a full chapter.

5. Build on Momentum:

Use each success as a stepping stone to tackle bigger challenges.

Example: After finishing a short course, enroll in an advanced program to deepen your skills.

Everyday Example of Small Wins

You want to declutter your home but feel overwhelmed. By starting with one drawer and completing it successfully, you build the momentum to tackle other areas.

Common Pitfalls in Small Wins

1. Neglecting Celebration:

Failing to recognize progress reduces motivation.

2. Getting Stuck on Minor Goals:

Focusing only on small wins without advancing toward the bigger picture stalls progress.

3. Expecting Immediate Results:

Small wins take time to accumulate into major successes.

Takeaway

Small wins create the momentum needed for big achievements. By focusing on incremental progress, celebrating successes, and building consistency, you turn daunting goals into attainable milestones.

Chapter 85: Combining Data and Intuition

What Does It Mean to Combine Data and Intuition?

Combining data and intuition involves using evidence-based insights alongside your gut feelings to make balanced decisions. Data provides objective clarity, while intuition offers personal judgment and creativity. Together, they create a comprehensive approach to complex decision-making.

Example:

A manager deciding on a marketing strategy analyzes campaign performance metrics (data) while considering how the audience might emotionally respond to specific content (intuition).

Why Balancing Data and Intuition Matters

1. Mitigates Bias:

Data helps counteract emotional biases, while intuition fills in gaps where data is incomplete.

2. Enhances Creativity:

Relying on both logic and instinct leads to more innovative solutions.

3. Improves Flexibility:

Intuition adapts quickly to changing circumstances, while data ensures choices remain grounded in facts.

Example:

An investor uses financial forecasts to guide their decisions (data) but follows their instincts about which industries are likely to grow in the future (intuition).

How to Combine Data and Intuition

1. Start with Data:

Collect and analyze relevant information to understand the situation clearly.

Example: A company looks at sales trends before deciding to launch a new product line.

2. Acknowledge Limitations:

Recognize that data may not capture every nuance, leaving room for judgment.

Example: While analytics show customer demand, the company relies on intuition to predict long-term trends.

3. Tune Your Intuition:

Build intuition through experience and reflection, making it a reliable complement to data.

Example: A chef knows from years of cooking when a recipe "feels right" even if they're experimenting with new techniques.

4. Test Assumptions:

Use data to validate or challenge your instincts, and adjust accordingly.

Example: A job seeker might feel an offer isn't right but compares the salary to market averages to confirm their gut feeling.

5. Balance Risks and Rewards:

Weigh both quantitative insights and qualitative factors to make well-rounded choices.

Example: A non-profit launching a campaign analyzes donation trends but also considers the emotional appeal of their messaging.

Everyday Example of Balancing Data and Intuition

You're choosing a new car. Data shows that a particular model has excellent safety ratings and fuel efficiency, but your intuition prefers a different model because it feels more comfortable and practical for your needs.

Common Pitfalls in Combining Data and Intuition

1. Overreliance on Data:

Excessive focus on numbers can ignore emotional or contextual factors.

2. Trusting Unrefined Instincts:

Intuition based on inexperience or incomplete knowledge may lead to errors.

3. Failing to Integrate Both:

Treating data and intuition as separate tools rather than complementary parts limits decision quality.

Takeaway

Combining data and intuition creates a balanced, effective approach to decision-making. By grounding choices in evidence while trusting refined instincts, you can navigate complexity with confidence and creativity.

Chapter 86: Meta-Decisions

What Are Meta-Decisions?

Meta-decisions are decisions about how to make decisions. They involve choosing the right process, tools, or mindset for solving a problem before diving into the specifics. This approach ensures your decision-making method aligns with the complexity and stakes of the situation.

Example:

A business deciding whether to launch a product chooses to rely on data analysis and market research, ensuring an informed process for the high-stakes decision.

Why Meta-Decisions Matter

1. Clarify Processes:

Deciding how to decide avoids confusion and aligns everyone involved on the right approach.

2. Save Time:

Meta-decisions streamline the process by focusing on the most effective method for the situation.

3. Improve Outcomes:

Tailoring your decision-making strategy to the problem ensures better results.

Example:

A family deciding on a vacation destination agrees to vote on options, ensuring fairness and efficiency in the process.

How to Make Meta-Decisions

1. Assess the Stakes:

Determine the importance and complexity of the decision to guide your approach.

Example: High-stakes financial decisions might require extensive research, while routine ones may rely on intuition.

2. Choose the Right Tools:

Select frameworks like decision trees, cost-benefit analysis, or brainstorming sessions based on the problem.

Example: A team uses a pros-and-cons list for a quick hiring decision but conducts thorough panel interviews for a leadership role.

3. Involve the Right People:

Decide who should contribute to the decision, considering expertise and stakeholder impact.

Example: A company includes IT staff in a decision about upgrading technology systems.

4. Define Success Metrics:

Establish criteria for evaluating the decision to ensure clarity.

Example: A non-profit defines success as increasing donations by 15% before choosing a campaign strategy.

5. Remain Flexible:

Be prepared to adjust your approach if the situation evolves or new information emerges.

Example: A couple initially planning to buy a home shifts to renting after market conditions change.

Everyday Example of Meta-Decisions

You're hosting a group dinner. Before deciding on a menu, you choose to poll guests about dietary restrictions and preferences, ensuring the final decision is inclusive.

Common Pitfalls in Meta-Decisions

1. Overthinking the Process:

Spending too much time deciding how to decide delays action.

2. Using the Wrong Approach:

Applying complex methods to simple problems wastes time and resources.

3. Failing to Adapt:

Sticking rigidly to an initial approach ignores evolving circumstances.

Takeaway

Meta-decisions create a foundation for smarter, more effective choices by defining the process before addressing the problem. By assessing stakes, selecting tools, and involving the right people, you can approach any decision with clarity and confidence.

Chapter 87: Information Overload

What Is Information Overload?

Information overload occurs when the sheer volume of data, opinions, and inputs becomes overwhelming, making it difficult to process, prioritize, and make decisions. Sifting through the noise to identify what's truly relevant ensures clarity and informed action.

Example:

A student researching a paper limits their sources to credible journals and avoids unrelated web results, streamlining their study process.

Why Avoiding Information Overload Matters

1. Improves Focus:

Filtering information reduces distractions, enabling you to concentrate on key issues.

2. Speeds Up Decisions:

Simplifying data reduces analysis paralysis and accelerates the decision-making process.

3. Enhances Decision Quality:

Focusing on high-quality, relevant information leads to better outcomes.

Example:

A professional choosing a software platform ignores marketing hype and focuses on user reviews and feature comparisons relevant to their needs.

How to Manage Information Overload

1. Define Your Goals:

Clarify the purpose of your decision to determine what information is necessary.

Example: If researching a new car, focus only on safety ratings, reliability, and affordability.

2. Set Boundaries:

Limit the time spent on research or the number of sources consulted to prevent overloading.

Example: "I'll review three credible articles before deciding on a health insurance plan."

3. Evaluate Credibility:

Prioritize information from trusted, reliable sources over anecdotal or biased inputs.

Example: When considering medical advice, rely on recommendations from certified professionals rather than social media posts.

4. Organize Data:

Use tools like lists, charts, or summaries to distill large amounts of information into clear insights.

Example: A homeowner compares contractors by listing costs, timelines, and reviews in a spreadsheet.

5. Eliminate Noise:

Avoid unnecessary inputs like irrelevant emails, social media, or excessive news updates during decision-making.

Example: Turn off notifications while evaluating investment options.

Everyday Example of Managing Information Overload

You're buying a smartphone. Instead of diving into endless reviews and specs, you decide on three key features (battery life, camera quality, and price) and only research models that meet these criteria.

Common Pitfalls in Managing Information Overload

1. Consuming Everything:

Trying to process all available information leads to confusion and delays.

2. Overvaluing Quantity Over Quality:

More data isn't better if it's not relevant or reliable.

3. Ignoring Actionable Insights:

Focusing on abstract data instead of actionable takeaways stalls progress.

Takeaway

Managing information overload is essential for clear, effective decision-making. By defining goals, filtering data, and focusing on relevance, you can sift through the noise to find clarity and confidence in your choices.

Decision Journals

Chapter 88: Decision Journals

What Are Decision Journals?

Decision journals are tools for recording the details of your decisions, including the reasoning behind them, anticipated outcomes, and eventual results. By reflecting on these entries, you identify patterns, refine your thought process, and improve future decisions.

Example:

A manager documents their reasoning for hiring a candidate, tracks their performance over six months, and evaluates whether the decision aligned with initial expectations.

Why Decision Journals Matter

1. Enhance Self-Awareness:

Journals reveal patterns in your thinking, highlighting strengths and areas for improvement.

2. Provide Accountability:

Writing down decisions forces you to articulate and justify your reasoning clearly.

3. Encourage Learning:

Reviewing outcomes helps you learn from successes and failures.

Example:

A person tracking their financial decisions realizes they frequently overestimate their ability to save, prompting adjustments to their budgeting habits.

How to Use Decision Journals

1. Record the Context:

Note the situation, the decision made, and any relevant constraints or goals.

Example: "I chose to invest in Stock A because it aligns with my long-term growth strategy."

2. Document Your Reasoning:

Include the factors that influenced your choice, such as data, intuition, or advice.

Example: "The company's revenue has grown 20% annually, and analysts project continued growth."

3. Predict Outcomes:

Write down what you expect to happen as a result of your decision.

Example: "I anticipate a 10% return within the next year."

4. Review Results:

After the decision plays out, evaluate whether the outcome matched your expectations and why.

Example: "The stock underperformed due to unexpected industry changes. Next time, I'll diversify more."

5. Identify Lessons Learned:

Reflect on how the experience can inform future choices.

Example: "This taught me to factor in external risks even when company fundamentals look strong."

Everyday Example of Using Decision Journals

You document your reasons for choosing a specific diet plan, including your goals and expected results. After three months, you review whether the plan met your expectations and make adjustments based on your experience.

Common Pitfalls in Using Decision Journals

1. Inconsistent Use:

Skipping entries makes it harder to identify patterns or learn from decisions.

2. Focusing Only on Successes:

Ignoring failures limits your ability to improve.

3. Overcomplicating the Process:

Journals should be simple enough to maintain consistently.

Takeaway

Decision journals transform decision-making into a continuous learning process. By tracking choices, reflecting on outcomes, and identifying lessons, you develop a more effective and self-aware approach to making decisions.

Chapter 89: When to Delegate

What Does It Mean to Delegate Decisions?

Delegation means entrusting tasks or decisions to others who are capable of handling them, freeing up your time and mental energy for higher-priority responsibilities. Knowing when and how to delegate ensures you leverage the strengths of your team or network effectively.

Example:

A manager delegates routine data entry to an assistant, allowing them to focus on strategic planning for an upcoming project.

Why Delegating Decisions Matters

1. Saves Time and Energy:

Delegation reduces your workload, preventing burnout and improving efficiency.

2. Increases Productivity:

Assigning tasks to those with relevant expertise often yields better results.

3. Builds Trust:

Empowering others to make decisions fosters collaboration and confidence.

Example:

A parent asks their teenager to plan the family's weekend outing, building decision-making skills while reducing stress for the parent.

How to Delegate Decisions Effectively

1. Identify Tasks to Delegate:

Focus on decisions that don't require your direct input or are outside your expertise.

Example: Delegate creating a project timeline to a colleague skilled in scheduling.

2. Choose the Right Person:

Assign tasks to individuals with the skills, experience, and capacity to handle them.

Example: A restaurant owner delegates menu design to their creative team rather than managing it personally.

3. Communicate Clearly:

Provide clear instructions, expectations, and any necessary resources.

Example: "Your goal is to research and recommend three vendors by Friday. Here are the criteria we need to meet."

4. Empower Decision-Making:

Allow the person to make their own choices within defined parameters.

Example: "You can choose the vendor, as long as the cost stays within our budget and they meet our quality standards."

5. Review and Support:

Check progress periodically and offer guidance as needed, without micromanaging.

Example: "How's the research coming along? Let me know if you need help narrowing down the options."

Everyday Example of Delegation

You're hosting a party and ask a friend to handle the playlist while another organizes food delivery. This delegation lets you focus on greeting guests and managing the overall flow of the event.

Common Pitfalls in Delegation

1. Micromanaging:

Over-involvement undermines the purpose of delegating and reduces trust.

2. Delegating Without Clarity:

Failing to provide clear expectations leads to confusion and subpar results.

3. Avoiding Delegation Entirely:

Trying to do everything yourself can lead to burnout and missed opportunities for collaboration.

Takeaway

Delegating decisions allows you to focus on high-priority tasks while empowering others to contribute their strengths. By choosing the right person, communicating clearly, and trusting the process, you build a more efficient and collaborative environment.

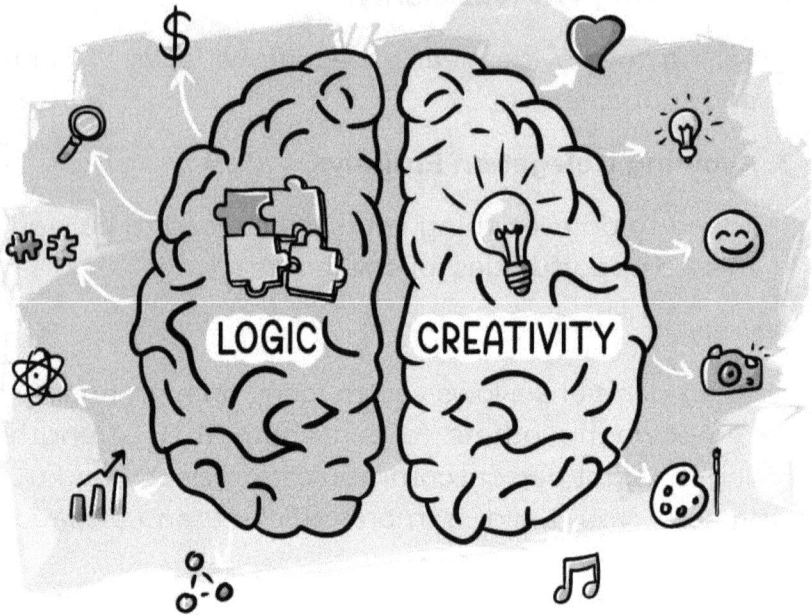

Chapter 90: Balancing Rationality and Creativity

What Does It Mean to Balance Rationality and Creativity?

Balancing rationality and creativity means combining logical analysis with imaginative thinking to develop effective and innovative solutions. Rationality grounds your decisions in facts and structure, while creativity generates fresh ideas and unique approaches.

Example:

An architect uses rationality to meet safety standards and budget constraints while employing creativity to design an inspiring, functional space.

Why Balancing Rationality and Creativity Matters

1. Encourages Innovation:

Creative thinking generates novel solutions, while rationality ensures feasibility.

2. Improves Problem-Solving:

Combining both approaches helps you address challenges from multiple angles.

3. Boosts Adaptability:

Creative solutions allow you to respond flexibly, while rational analysis provides stability.

Example:

A startup designing a marketing campaign combines data on customer preferences (rationality) with bold, eye-catching content (creativity).

How to Balance Rationality and Creativity

1. Start with Structure:

Use rational thinking to define the problem, set goals, and gather data.

Example: A teacher identifies that students struggle with engagement during lessons.

2. Brainstorm Freely:

Encourage creative ideas without judgment to explore unconventional solutions.

Example: The teacher considers using interactive games, storytelling, or role-playing to make lessons more engaging.

3. Test and Refine:

Evaluate creative ideas using rational criteria like feasibility, cost, and impact.

Example: The teacher implements role-playing, measures engagement, and refines the approach based on feedback.

4. Embrace Iteration:

Alternate between rational and creative modes to improve and adapt your solutions.

Example: A product designer prototypes an idea, gathers user feedback, and iterates with both logic and imagination.

5. Collaborate for Balance:

Involve diverse perspectives to integrate logical and creative strengths.

Example: A scientist and artist work together on an educational exhibit, blending technical accuracy with engaging visuals.

Everyday Example of Balancing Rationality and Creativity

You're organizing a fundraiser. Rationality helps you set a budget and logistics, while creativity inspires unique themes and interactive activities to draw attendees.

Common Pitfalls in Balancing Rationality and Creativity

1. Overemphasizing Logic:

Rigid thinking stifles creativity and limits innovative potential.

2. Relying Solely on Creativity:

Ignoring practical constraints can make ideas unrealistic or ineffective.

3. Forgetting to Iterate:

Stopping at the first idea misses opportunities for improvement.

Takeaway

Balancing rationality and creativity enables you to solve problems innovatively. By grounding ideas in logic while allowing room for imagination, you create solutions that are both practical and inspired.

Part X: Building a Decision-Making Framework

Great decision-making isn't just about individual choices; it's about creating a system. This section equips you with tools to build a framework that ensures clarity, consistency, and adaptability in your decision-making process. By developing guiding principles, learning from feedback, and fostering self-awareness, you can make confident decisions in any situation.

Chapter 91: The Decision-Making Code

What Is the Decision-Making Code?

The decision-making code is a personal set of guiding principles that align your choices with your values and goals. It acts as a compass, helping you navigate complexity and make consistent, purpose-driven decisions.

Example:

A leader with a guiding principle of transparency ensures open communication with their team, even during challenging times.

Why Developing Guiding Principles Matters

1. Ensures Consistency:

A clear code eliminates guesswork and keeps decisions aligned with your values.

2. Simplifies Complex Choices:

Principles provide a foundation for evaluating options, reducing overwhelm.

3. Builds Confidence:

Knowing your decisions align with your values fosters trust in your process.

Example:

A business owner prioritizes sustainability, choosing vendors and practices that reflect this value, even if it costs more initially.

How to Develop Your Decision-Making Code

1. Identify Your Core Values:

Reflect on what matters most to you, such as honesty, growth, or balance.

Example: "I value fairness, so I'll prioritize equitable outcomes in my decisions."

2. Define Your Principles:

Translate values into actionable statements to guide choices.

Example: "Always prioritize long-term gains over short-term fixes."

3. Test Your Principles:

Apply them to past decisions to ensure they hold up in real scenarios.

Example: "Would this principle have helped me avoid a past mistake?"

4. Adapt as Needed:

Revise your code as your goals and circumstances evolve.

Example: A parent might adjust their principles to include flexibility as their children grow older.

5. Document and Review:

Write down your principles and revisit them regularly to reinforce their impact.

Example: Keep a journal where you list principles and how they've guided key decisions.

Everyday Example of a Decision-Making Code

You're deciding whether to switch jobs. Your principle of prioritizing work-life balance helps you choose a role that offers remote work and flexible hours over one with higher pay but longer hours.

Common Pitfalls in Developing a Decision-Making Code

1. Being Too Vague:

Broad principles like "Do good" lack actionable guidance.

2. Ignoring Values:

A code that doesn't reflect your true priorities leads to inconsistency.

3. Failing to Revisit Principles:

Outdated principles may no longer align with your current life goals.

Takeaway

A decision-making code anchors your choices in purpose and clarity. By defining and refining your guiding principles, you create a consistent framework for navigating even the most complex situations.

Chapter 92: Consistency Over Perfection

What Does Consistency Over Perfection Mean?

Consistency over perfection is the principle of focusing on steady, reliable progress rather than trying to make flawless decisions every time. It's about valuing action and learning from mistakes instead of being paralyzed by fear of failure.

Example:

Instead of obsessing over the perfect workout plan, someone commits to exercising 30 minutes a day, knowing consistency matters more than precision.

Why Consistency Matters More Than Perfection

1. Builds Momentum:

Regular effort leads to cumulative success, even if every step isn't perfect.

2. Encourages Experimentation:

A focus on progress allows you to test ideas without fearing mistakes.

3. Reduces Stress:

Letting go of perfectionism creates a healthier, more productive mindset.

Example:

A writer commits to drafting 500 words a day, improving their skills over time instead of waiting for perfect inspiration.

How to Prioritize Consistency

1. Set Small, Achievable Goals:

Focus on incremental progress to maintain motivation.

Example: Instead of aiming to lose 20 pounds immediately, set a goal to lose 2 pounds a month.

2. Embrace Imperfection:

Accept that mistakes are part of the process and opportunities to learn.

Example: A baker tests new recipes, knowing some attempts will fail but refine their skills.

3. Create Habits:

Build routines that support consistent action.

Example: Schedule 15 minutes daily for language practice instead of trying to cram before a trip.

4. Celebrate Milestones:

Acknowledge progress to reinforce the value of consistency.

Example: Reward yourself for completing a week of workouts, even if some sessions were shorter than planned.

5. Reflect and Adjust:

Regularly evaluate your progress and refine your approach.

Example: A student revises their study schedule after realizing they focus better in the morning.

Everyday Example of Consistency Over Perfection

You're learning to play guitar. Instead of aiming for flawless performances, you practice for 10 minutes daily, gradually building confidence and skill.

Common Pitfalls in Prioritizing Consistency

1. Expecting Quick Results:

Impatience can lead to frustration and quitting.

2. Letting Setbacks Derail Progress:

Missing one day of effort doesn't mean abandoning your goal entirely.

3. Overcommitting:

Setting unsustainable goals undermines consistency.

Takeaway

Consistency over perfection focuses on steady growth, turning small, repeated efforts into lasting success. By prioritizing progress and embracing imperfection, you create a resilient framework for achieving your goals.

Chapter 93: Feedback Loops

What Are Feedback Loops?

Feedback loops are systems for gathering information about the outcomes of your decisions and using that data to improve future choices. Whether positive or negative, feedback provides actionable insights that refine your decision-making process.

Example:

A manager launches a new team workflow and gathers input from employees after a month. Based on their feedback, they adjust timelines and tools to improve efficiency.

Why Feedback Loops Matter

1. Encourage Continuous Growth:

Feedback helps you adapt and evolve, making each decision better than the last.

2. Reveal Blind Spots:

Input from others highlights areas you might overlook on your own.

3. Boost Decision Quality:

Regular refinement ensures your strategies remain effective over time.

Example:

A musician performing live tracks audience reactions and adjusts their setlist to include more popular songs.

How to Use Feedback Loops Effectively

1. Invite Honest Input:

Create a safe environment where others feel comfortable sharing constructive feedback.

Example: A teacher asks students to complete anonymous surveys about class effectiveness.

2. Evaluate Outcomes:

Regularly analyze the results of your decisions to identify what worked and what didn't.

Example: A runner tracks their training progress to adjust their regimen for better performance.

3. Refine and Repeat:

Apply feedback to improve your approach, then test it again.

Example: A small business adjusts its pricing strategy based on customer feedback and monitors sales trends to measure the impact.

4. Focus on Patterns:

Look for recurring themes in feedback to address underlying issues.

Example: A project manager notices consistent complaints about communication gaps and implements regular status updates.

5. Avoid Overreacting to Outliers:

Balance individual feedback with broader trends to avoid making knee-jerk changes.

Example: A restaurant owner considers overall customer reviews instead of focusing on one particularly harsh critique.

Everyday Example of Feedback Loops

You're learning to cook a new dish. After each attempt, you note what went well and what didn't, adjusting the recipe until you perfect it.

Common Pitfalls in Feedback Loops

1. Ignoring Feedback:

Dismissing input undermines growth and perpetuates mistakes.

2. Taking Feedback Personally:

Viewing criticism as an attack rather than an opportunity stifles improvement.

3. Making Changes Too Quickly:

Overreacting to isolated feedback can disrupt effective strategies.

Takeaway

Feedback loops are essential for continuous learning and refinement. By seeking input, evaluating outcomes, and applying lessons learned, you create a dynamic system that improves your decision-making over time.

Chapter 94: Self-Awareness Practices

What Are Self-Awareness Practices?

Self-awareness practices are techniques that help you understand your thoughts, emotions, and behavior patterns. By recognizing these patterns, you can identify biases, play to your strengths, and make decisions aligned with your true priorities.

Example:

A professional reflects on their habit of procrastination and adopts time-blocking to improve productivity.

Why Self-Awareness Matters

1. Reveals Hidden Biases:

Understanding your cognitive tendencies reduces errors in judgment.

2. Enhances Emotional Regulation:

Awareness of your triggers helps you respond calmly under pressure.

3. Improves Alignment with Goals:

Self-awareness ensures your actions reflect your long-term objectives.

Example:

An athlete notices their tendency to self-criticize and replaces negative self-talk with affirmations, improving performance and confidence.

How to Cultivate Self-Awareness

1. Keep a Decision Journal:

Track your choices and outcomes to identify recurring patterns and areas for growth.

Example: Log decisions about finances and analyze whether they align with your savings goals.

2. Practice Mindfulness:

Focus on the present moment to recognize thoughts and emotions without judgment.

Example: During a tense meeting, take deep breaths to observe your reactions instead of acting impulsively.

3. Seek Feedback:

Ask trusted peers for insights into how they perceive your behavior or decisions.

Example: "Do you think I'm too quick to dismiss alternative ideas in meetings?"

4. Reflect Regularly:

Set aside time to review your day, noting what went well and what could improve.

Example: Use a nightly journal to jot down three successes and one lesson learned.

5. Identify Your Triggers:

Recognize situations that lead to poor decisions, and develop strategies to manage them.

Example: If stress leads you to overspend, create a budget to guide decisions during high-pressure times.

Everyday Example of Self-Awareness Practices

You notice that hunger often makes you irritable and prone to snap decisions. Keeping healthy snacks on hand helps you stay balanced and make better choices.

Common Pitfalls in Self-Awareness

1. Avoiding Reflection:

Ignoring your patterns prevents growth and perpetuates mistakes.

2. Overanalyzing:

Dwelling excessively on flaws can lead to paralysis rather than improvement.

3. Resisting Feedback:

Rejecting others' observations limits your ability to see blind spots.

Takeaway

Self-awareness is a cornerstone of effective decision-making. By recognizing your patterns, managing emotions, and aligning actions with goals, you become more intentional and confident in your choices.

Chapter 95: The Experimenter's Mindset

What Is the Experimenter's Mindset?

The experimenter's mindset treats life as a series of experiments, where each decision is a hypothesis tested through action. Successes validate your ideas, while failures provide valuable lessons. This approach encourages curiosity, adaptability, and continuous improvement.

Example:

A professional tests new productivity methods like time-blocking or task batching, refining their workflow based on results.

Why the Experimenter's Mindset Matters

1. Reduces Fear of Failure:

Viewing mistakes as data removes the emotional sting of failure.

2. Encourages Innovation:

Experimentation leads to discoveries you might not reach through conventional thinking.

3. Fosters Adaptability:

Iterative testing prepares you to adjust strategies in response to new information.

Example:

A person trying to improve their diet experiments with meal prepping one week and intuitive eating the next, learning what works best for their lifestyle.

How to Adopt the Experimenter's Mindset

1. Frame Decisions as Hypotheses:

Define what you want to test and what you expect to learn.

Example: "If I spend 10 minutes meditating daily, I'll feel more focused by the end of the week."

2. Start Small:

Test ideas on a manageable scale to reduce risk and gather insights quickly.

Example: Before committing to a career change, take a short course in the field to gauge your interest.

3. Measure Results:

Track outcomes to determine whether the experiment achieved its goals.

Example: A business tracks customer engagement after introducing a new email marketing strategy.

4. Embrace Iteration:

Use results to refine your approach and run further tests.

Example: Adjust your exercise routine based on what energizes you most during the day.

5. Stay Curious:

Treat every outcome as an opportunity to learn, whether it confirms or challenges your hypothesis.

Example: If a strategy doesn't work, ask, "Why?" and explore alternatives.

Everyday Example of the Experimenter's Mindset

You're looking for ways to save money on groceries. One week, you try shopping at a discount store; the next, you focus on meal planning. Comparing the results helps you identify the most effective strategy.

Common Pitfalls in Experimentation

1. Expecting Instant Success:

Not all experiments yield immediate or clear results.

2. Fearing Mistakes:

Avoiding risks stifles opportunities for growth and discovery.

3. Ignoring Lessons Learned:

Failing to analyze results misses the point of experimentation.

Takeaway

The experimenter's mindset transforms decisions into opportunities for growth. By testing hypotheses, learning from outcomes, and iterating your approach, you can turn curiosity into actionable insights that drive continuous improvement.

Chapter 96: Reverse Engineering Success

What Is Reverse Engineering Success?

Reverse engineering success means analyzing the achievements of role models or organizations to identify the steps, strategies, and principles they followed. By understanding how they reached their goals, you can create your own roadmap for similar success.

Example:

An aspiring entrepreneur studies the growth strategies of a successful start-up to apply relevant tactics to their own business.

Why Reverse Engineering Matters

1. Provides Proven Strategies:

Learning from others saves time and avoids reinventing the wheel.

2. Inspires Action:

Seeing how others achieved their goals makes your own ambitions feel more attainable.

3. Customizes Your Approach:

Adapting successful methods to your unique situation ensures relevance and effectiveness.

Example:

A musician analyzing how their favorite artist built an audience on social media adapts similar engagement tactics to grow their fan base.

How to Reverse Engineer Success

1. Identify Role Models:

Choose individuals or organizations whose achievements align with your goals.

Example: A writer examines the habits of bestselling authors to improve their own workflow.

2. Study Their Process:

Break down the steps, decisions, and milestones that contributed to their success.

Example: A non-profit analyzes how a similar organization grew donations through targeted campaigns.

3. Focus on Key Principles:

Look for underlying strategies rather than copying surface-level actions.

Example: Instead of mimicking a celebrity's exact workout routine, focus on their discipline and consistency.

4. Adapt to Your Context:

Adjust lessons learned to fit your resources, strengths, and challenges.

Example: A start-up tailors an established company's customer service practices to suit their smaller team.

5. Track Progress:

Measure how applying these strategies impacts your own outcomes.

Example: A student adopting a successful study technique monitors results.

Everyday Example of Reverse Engineering Success

You admire a colleague's ability to manage time effectively. By observing their use of calendars, task prioritization, and delegation, you adopt similar practices to streamline your own schedule.

Common Pitfalls in Reverse Engineering

1. Blindly Copying:

Mimicking actions without understanding the reasoning behind them leads to superficial results.

2. Ignoring Context:

Failing to adapt strategies to your unique situation limits their effectiveness.

3. Focusing Only on Outcomes:

Overlooking the hard work and setbacks behind success creates unrealistic expectations.

Takeaway

Reverse engineering success offers a practical way to learn from others' achievements. By analyzing strategies, focusing on key principles, and adapting them to your context, you can create a customized path to your goals.

Chapter 97: Embracing Complexity

What Does It Mean to Embrace Complexity?

Embracing complexity means accepting uncertainty, interconnected factors, and ever-changing conditions as part of decision-making. It involves thinking dynamically, staying flexible, and focusing on the bigger picture to navigate challenges effectively.

Example:

A CEO facing a volatile market adopts multiple strategies, balancing cost-cutting measures with investment in innovation to adapt to unpredictable conditions.

Why Embracing Complexity Matters

1. Encourages Resilience:

Recognizing that uncertainty is unavoidable helps you adapt instead of resisting change.

2. Reveals Hidden Opportunities:

Complex situations often present chances for innovation and growth.

3. Improves Strategic Thinking:

Viewing problems from multiple angles enables well-rounded solutions.

Example:

A nonprofit navigating shifting funding priorities explores diverse revenue streams to maintain stability and expand impact.

How to Embrace Complexity

1. Shift Your Mindset:

See complexity as an opportunity for growth, not a barrier.

Example: "How can this challenge teach me to approach problems differently?"

2. Break Down the Problem:

Divide complex issues into smaller, manageable components to identify key factors.

Example: A project manager addressing delays categorizes issues into communication, resource allocation, and technical bottlenecks.

3. Focus on Interconnections:

Analyze how various elements interact and influence one another.

Example: A city planner evaluates how housing policies impact transportation, employment, and public health.

4. Prepare for Multiple Outcomes:

Anticipate a range of scenarios and develop flexible strategies.

Example: An investor creates a diversified portfolio to hedge against market uncertainty.

5. Practice Adaptive Thinking:

Stay open to revising your approach as new information emerges.

Example: A teacher adjusts their lesson plan mid-class based on student engagement levels.

Everyday Example of Embracing Complexity

You're planning a wedding but encounter unexpected challenges, like a venue cancellation. By staying flexible, you consider alternative options and prioritize what truly matters, ensuring a meaningful celebration.

Common Pitfalls in Complex Decision-Making

1. Oversimplifying Problems:

Ignoring interconnected factors can lead to ineffective solutions.

2. Freezing Under Pressure:

Complexity can overwhelm, leading to inaction.

3. Focusing Solely on Short-Term Fixes:

Quick solutions often fail to address root causes.

Takeaway

Embracing complexity equips you to navigate uncertainty with confidence and adaptability. By breaking problems into manageable parts, analyzing interconnections, and staying open to change, you turn ambiguity into opportunity.

Chapter 98: The Continuous Learner

What Does It Mean to Be a Continuous Learner?

A continuous learner actively seeks knowledge, skills, and perspectives to refine their understanding and decision-making abilities. This mindset embraces curiosity as a driving force for growth, adaptability, and lifelong improvement.

Example:

A software developer stays ahead of industry trends by learning new programming languages, ensuring their expertise remains relevant.

Why Lifelong Learning Matters

1. Enhances Problem-Solving:

Expanding your knowledge equips you with diverse tools and perspectives.

2. Builds Resilience:

Learning fosters adaptability, helping you navigate changes and challenges.

3. Encourages Innovation:

Curiosity leads to fresh ideas and creative solutions.

Example:

A business leader reads books on psychology, technology, and leadership to inform better strategies and inspire their team.

How to Foster Continuous Learning

1. Stay Curious:

Approach situations with a mindset of exploration and discovery.

Example: "What can I learn from this challenge, even if it seems small?"

2. Seek Diverse Inputs:

Expose yourself to different fields, cultures, and ideas to broaden your perspective.

Example: A scientist attends art workshops to inspire creative approaches to research.

3. Reflect Regularly:

Review what you've learned and how it applies to your decisions.

Example: Keep a journal of new skills or insights gained from daily experiences.

4. Invest in Education:

Take courses, read books, or attend seminars to deepen your expertise.

Example: A marketer enrolls in a data analytics course to enhance campaign strategies.

5. Learn from Others:

Engage with mentors, peers, and diverse communities to share knowledge.

Example: Join a networking group to exchange insights and expand your horizons.

Everyday Example of Continuous Learning

You're interested in gardening but have no experience. By watching tutorials, experimenting with plants, and seeking advice, you develop a thriving garden and a rewarding new hobby.

Common Pitfalls in Lifelong Learning

1. Avoiding New Challenges:

Sticking to familiar areas limits growth opportunities.

2. Overloading with Information:

Focusing on too many topics at once can dilute learning efforts.

3. Failing to Apply Knowledge:

Learning without action doesn't translate into meaningful improvement.

Takeaway

Continuous learning fuels better decision-making by equipping you with diverse skills and perspectives. By staying curious, seeking knowledge, and applying what you learn, you grow into a more adaptive and innovative decision-maker.

Chapter 99: Legacy Decisions

What Are Legacy Decisions?

Legacy decisions are choices made with the intention of leaving a lasting positive impact on future generations, your community, or the world. These decisions reflect your values and prioritize long-term benefits over short-term gains.

Example:

A philanthropist invests in educational scholarships, knowing their contribution will empower students for decades to come.

Why Legacy Decisions Matter

1. Extend Your Influence:

Legacy decisions allow your actions to create a ripple effect that benefits others long after you're gone.

2. Align with Purpose:

Thinking beyond immediate outcomes connects your choices to meaningful goals and values.

3. Promote Sustainability:

Long-term thinking ensures that resources and opportunities are preserved for future generations.

Example:

A company commits to reducing its carbon footprint by adopting sustainable practices, balancing profits with environmental responsibility.

How to Make Legacy Decisions

1. Define Your Legacy Goals:

Reflect on what impact you want to leave behind, whether it's personal, professional, or societal.

Example: "I want to contribute to environmental conservation by supporting reforestation projects."

2. Think Long-Term:

Evaluate how your decisions will affect future generations or stakeholders.

Example: A parent chooses to teach their children financial literacy, ensuring they have tools for lifelong stability.

3. Invest in Meaningful Projects:

Focus your time, money, or energy on initiatives that align with your values and have enduring impact.

Example: An entrepreneur mentors young startups, fostering innovation and community growth.

4. Collaborate for Greater Impact:

Work with others who share your vision to amplify the results of your efforts.

Example: A local leader forms partnerships to improve public transportation in underserved areas.

5. Regularly Revisit Your Legacy Goals:

As your circumstances and priorities evolve, adjust your decisions to stay aligned with your values.

Example: A retiree shifts from career-focused goals to philanthropic endeavors that promote equity and education.

Everyday Example of Legacy Decisions

You start a small community garden in your neighborhood. While it benefits residents today, it also teaches future generations about sustainability and teamwork.

Common Pitfalls in Legacy Decisions

1. Overlooking Immediate Needs:

Focusing too much on the future may neglect pressing current issues.

2. Underestimating Small Actions:

Assuming that only grand gestures matter limits your ability to create lasting change.

3. Failing to Inspire Others:

A legacy is more effective when shared with and embraced by others.

Takeaway

Legacy decisions prioritize long-term impact and reflect your deepest values. By aligning your choices with a purpose, collaborating with others, and thinking about future generations, you create a meaningful legacy that transcends your lifetime.

Chapter 100: Master Your Mindset

What Does It Mean to Master Your Mindset?

Mastering your mindset means cultivating the habits, perspectives, and emotional resilience needed to make sound, confident decisions. It's about blending rationality with empathy, focusing on growth, and staying adaptable in the face of challenges.

Example:

A leader faced with a tough decision balances data-driven analysis with a genuine understanding of how their choice will affect team morale.

Why Mindset Matters in Decision-Making

1. Enhances Confidence:

A strong mindset reduces hesitation and builds trust in your process.

2. Promotes Adaptability:

A growth-oriented outlook helps you pivot effectively when circumstances change.

3. Encourages Consistency:

Habits grounded in self-awareness and reflection lead to more reliable outcomes.

Example:

A student adopting a "fail-forward" mindset learns from mistakes and continues improving instead of giving up after setbacks.

The Habits of Great Decision-Makers

1. Seek Clarity:

Ask focused questions and gather relevant information before acting.

Example: A negotiator outlines clear objectives and goals before entering discussions.

2. Embrace Reflection:

Regularly review past decisions to identify strengths and areas for growth.

Example: A teacher reflects on classroom strategies each semester to refine their methods.

3. Balance Logic and Emotion:

Integrate rational analysis with empathy and intuition for well-rounded choices.

Example: A parent deciding on a move considers both financial benefits and emotional effects on their children.

4. Stay Curious:

Approach every situation as an opportunity to learn and grow.

Example: A designer experiments with new tools and techniques to enhance creativity and problem-solving.

5. Practice Patience:

Avoid rushing decisions when careful thought is required, but act decisively when the moment calls for it.

Example: A firefighter evaluates risks quickly during an emergency but remains calm under pressure.

Everyday Example of a Mastered Mindset

You're deciding on a significant career change. By gathering data, reflecting on your values, considering long-term effects, and consulting trusted advisors, you confidently make a decision that aligns with both your goals and well-being.

Common Pitfalls in Mindset Mastery

1. Overthinking Decisions:

Focusing excessively on perfection delays necessary action.

2. Reacting Emotionally:

Allowing temporary emotions to dominate leads to regretful choices.

3. Ignoring Growth Opportunities:

Avoiding challenges out of fear limits personal and professional development.

Takeaway

Mastering your mindset is the key to becoming a great decision-maker. By cultivating habits like reflection, balance, curiosity, and patience, you can navigate life's challenges with confidence, resilience, and clarity.

Conclusion: The AI Perspective

Decision-making is an art shaped by human emotions, instincts, and experiences. But what if you could approach decisions with the precision and adaptability of artificial intelligence?

Beyond Instinct: How Thinking Like an AI Can Reshape Human Decisions

Humans often lean on instinct and emotions — powerful tools evolved for survival. Yet, in today's complex world, these tools can sometimes fail us, leading to biases, snap judgments, and regrettable choices. Thinking like an AI doesn't mean erasing instinct—it means augmenting it with clarity, logic, and adaptability.

Here's how adopting an AI-inspired approach can reshape your decisions:

1. Focus on Data Over Assumptions:

AI analyzes facts, patterns, and probabilities, bypassing emotional shortcuts. Similarly, you can ground your choices in evidence, challenging assumptions and seeking clarity.

Example: Instead of assuming a decision is risky, gather data to assess the actual likelihood of success or failure.

2. Continuously Learn and Iterate:

AI refines itself with every input, improving over time. You can do the same by reflecting on outcomes, learning from mistakes, and applying those lessons to future decisions.

Example: Treating each failure as feedback turns setbacks into stepping stones for success.

3. Balance Speed and Precision:

AI excels at both rapid responses and deliberate analysis, depending on the situation. Adopting this dual mode allows you to act decisively when needed and think deeply when stakes are high.

Example: Use quick rules for routine choices and reserve thoughtful frameworks for strategic ones.

4. Embrace Objectivity with Empathy:

AI evaluates options without bias, but as a human, you can add empathy to the equation. Blending objectivity with compassion ensures that your decisions serve both logic and humanity.

Example: A leader uses data to evaluate a restructuring plan but also considers its emotional impact on employees.

By thinking like an AI, you transcend instinct while keeping the heart of human decision-making intact. It's not about replacing what makes you human — it's about elevating your abilities with tools of precision and adaptability.

Wisdom for the Decision-Maker's Journey

As you navigate life's twists and turns, remember these parting lessons:

1. Clarity is Key:

Clear decisions come from asking the right questions and seeking meaningful answers. When in doubt, simplify the problem to its core.

2. Balance Logic and Emotion:

Great decisions honor both your rational mind and emotional heart. Trust data, but listen to your intuition when it's rooted in experience.

3. Focus on the Long Term:

Short-term wins can feel gratifying, but meaningful success often requires patience and persistence. Keep your eyes on the bigger picture.

4. Learn, Adapt, and Evolve:

No decision is the final word. Each choice is a step forward—an opportunity to refine, improve, and make better decisions tomorrow.

5. Empower Others:

Decisions aren't made in isolation. Seek perspectives, collaborate, and trust others to contribute their strengths to shared goals.

The decision-making journey is not a straight path; it's a dynamic process shaped by reflection, action, and continuous learning. You now hold 100 strategies designed to sharpen your thinking, strengthen your resolve, and guide your choices. But the power to apply them lies in your hands.

Your best decisions aren't just ahead of you—they're within you, waiting to be realized. Take the first step boldly, with clarity, curiosity, and conviction.

Appendix A: Quick Reference Guide to 100 Strategies for Choosing Wisely When Human Instinct Fails

This appendix offers a short description of all 100 strategies, making it easy to recap the various models.

Part I: Foundations of Smart Decision-Making

1. **The Science of Choice:** Why human instincts often misfire.

2. **Logic vs. Emotion:** Finding the balance.

3. **The Anatomy of a Decision:** Understanding the process.

4. **The Role of Bias:** Identifying your blind spots.

5. **The Power of Awareness:** Recognizing when instinct falters.

6. **The AI Advantage:** Thinking beyond human intuition.

7. **Decision-Making in the Modern World:** Challenges and opportunities.

25. **Overconfidence Bias:** A dose of humility strengthens decisions.

26. **Framing Effect:** Reframe the problem for new perspectives.

27. **Loss Aversion:** Stop letting fear dictate your choices.

28. **Hindsight Bias:** Learn, don't judge the past.

29. **Groupthink:** Think independently in a crowd.

30. **Dunning-Kruger Effect:** Recognize when you don't know enough.

Part IV: Tools and Techniques for Rational Decision-Making

31. **The Decision Tree:** Map out your options.

32. **The Six Thinking Hats:** Approach problems from multiple angles.

33. **SWOT Analysis:** Weigh strengths, weaknesses, opportunities, and threats.

34. **Weighted Scoring:** Assign value to your priorities.

35. **Scenario Planning:** Prepare for every "what if."

36. **Pre-Mortem Analysis:** Imagine your decision failing— then fix it.

37. **Monte Carlo Simulation:** Model uncertainty for better predictions.

38. **Decision Matrices:** Simplify complex choices.

39. **Pro/Con Lists Done Right:** Add context to your lists.

40. **Heuristic Shortcuts:** Use them wisely to save time.

Part V: Emotional Intelligence in Decision-Making

41. **Self-Regulation:** Mastering emotional control.

42. **Empathy and Decisions:** Understand how others feel.

43. **The Role of Intuition:** When to trust your gut.

44. **Dealing with Decision Fatigue:** Stay sharp under pressure.

45. **Stress-Reduction Techniques:** Think clearly in chaos.

46. **The Pause Principle:** When in doubt, wait.

47. **Handling Regret:** Move forward gracefully.

48. **Mindfulness Practices:** Focus your mind for better outcomes.

49. **Cultivating Resilience:** Bounce back from failure.

50. **Making Peace with Uncertainty:** Embrace the unknown.

Part VI: Group and Team Decision-Making

51. **Consensus-Building:** Aligning diverse opinions.

52. **Avoiding Power Dynamics:** Keep decisions fair.

53. **The Wisdom of Crowds:** Leverage group intelligence.

54. **The Delphi Technique:** Structured collaboration for complex problems.

55. **Role Assignment:** Clarity in group responsibilities.

56. **Conflict Resolution Skills:** Handle disagreements productively.

57. **Decision Mapping for Teams:** Visualize shared choices.

58. **Encouraging Constructive Dissent:** Let disagreement

improve decisions.

59. **Combating Group Polarization:** Keep discussions balanced.

60. **Accountability in Groups:** Commit to follow-through.

Part VII: Strategic Thinking for Long-Term Success

61. **Game Theory Basics:** Anticipate others' moves.

62. **The Long View:** Align today's choices with future goals.

63. **Scenario Thinking:** Plan for multiple futures.

64. **Red Teaming:** Challenge your own decisions.

65. **Bets and Odds:** Think probabilistically.

66. **Competitive Analysis:** Understand rivals' strategies.

67. **The Timing Factor:** Act at the right moment.

68. **Avoiding Analysis Paralysis:** Know when to stop thinking.

69. **The Power of Experimentation:** Test your choices.

70. **Strategic Patience:** Wait for the right opportunities.

Part VIII: Everyday Decision-Making

71. **Choosing Careers:** Aligning passion and practicality.

72. **Financial Decisions:** Invest in what matters.

73. **Time Management:** Make every hour count.

74. **Health Choices:** Decisions that build well-being.

75. **Relationship Decisions:** Balancing logic and emotion.

76. **Parenting with Purpose:** Decision-making for families.

77. Buying Smart: Evaluate big purchases wisely.

78. Where to Live: Assess location choices effectively.

79. Handling Crises: Make decisions under pressure.

80. The Minimalist Mindset: Fewer choices, better outcomes.

Part IX: Advanced Decision-Making

81. Cognitive Load Management: Avoid mental overload.

82. Learning from Failure: Turn mistakes into strategies.

83. Bias Audits: Regularly review your thinking.

84. The Power of Small Wins: Build momentum.

85. Combining Data and Intuition: Balance the best of both worlds.

86. Meta-Decisions: How to decide how to decide.

87. Information Overload: Sift through noise for clarity.

88. Decision Journals: Track and refine your process.

89. When to Delegate: Let others decide for you.

90. Balancing Rationality and Creativity: Solve problems innovatively.

Part X: Building a Decision-Making Framework

91. The Decision-Making Code: Develop your guiding principles.

92. Consistency Over Perfection: Prioritize progress.

93. Feedback Loops: Learn and improve continuously.

94. Self-Awareness Practices: Stay tuned to your patterns.

95. The Experimenter's Mindset: Approach life as a lab.

96. Reverse Engineering Success: Learn from role models.

97. Embracing Complexity: Thrive in uncertain environments.

98. The Continuous Learner: Stay curious and adaptive.

99. Legacy Decisions: Thinking beyond your lifetime.

100. Master Your Mindset: The habits of great decision-makers.

Appendix B: 100 Strategies for Choosing Wisely by Category

This appendix organizes all 100 strategies into intuitive categories, making it easier to find the tools you need for specific challenges.

Foundations of Smart Decision-Making

- The Science of Choice
- Logic vs. Emotion
- The Anatomy of a Decision
- The Role of Bias
- The Power of Awareness
- The AI Advantage
- Decision-Making in the Modern World
- Defining Success in Decision-making
- The Decision-Making Blueprint
- Adaptability Matters

Mental Models for Superior Thinking

- First Principles Thinking
- Occam's Razor
- The Pareto Principle
- Second-Order Thinking
- Inversion
- Opportunity Cost
- The Eisenhower Matrix:
- Bayesian Thinking
- Regret Minimization
- The Fermi Approach

Strategies to Overcome Cognitive Biases

- Anchoring Bias
- Confirmation Bias
- Availability Heuristic
- Sunk Cost Fallacy
- Overconfidence Bias
- Framing Effect
- Loss Aversion
- Hindsight Bias
- Groupthink
- Dunning-Kruger Effect

Tools and Techniques for Rational Decision-Making

- The Decision Tree

- The Six Thinking Hats

- SWOT Analysis

- Weighted Scoring

- Scenario Planning

- Pre-Mortem Analysis

- Monte Carlo Simulation

- Decision Matrices

- Pro/Con Lists Done Right

- Heuristic Shortcuts

Emotional Intelligence in Decision-Making

- Self-Regulation

- Empathy and Decisions

- The Role of Intuition

- Dealing with Decision Fatigue

- Stress-Reduction Techniques

- The Pause Principle

- Handling Regret

- Mindfulness Practices

- Cultivating Resilience

- Making Peace with Uncertainty

Group and Team Decision-Making

- Consensus-Building
- Avoiding Power Dynamics
- The Wisdom of Crowds
- The Delphi Technique
- Role Assignment
- Conflict Resolution Skills
- Decision Mapping for Teams
- Encouraging Constructive Dissent
- Combating Group Polarization
- Accountability in Groups

Strategic Thinking for Long-Term Success

- Game Theory Basics
- The Long View
- Scenario Thinking
- Red Teaming
- Bets and Odds
- Competitive Analysis
- The Timing Factor
- Avoiding Analysis Paralysis
- The Power of Experimentation
- Strategic Patience

Everyday Decision-Making

- Choosing Careers
- Financial Decisions
- Time Management
- Health Choices
- Relationship Decisions
- Parenting with Purpose
- Buying Smart
- Where to Live
- Handling Crises
- The Minimalist Mindset

Advanced Decision-Making

- Cognitive Load Management
- Learning from Failure
- Bias Audits
- The Power of Small Wins
- Combining Data and Intuition
- Meta-Decisions
- Information Overload
- Decision Journals
- When to Delegate
- Balancing Rationality and Creativity

Building a Decision-Making Framework

- The Decision-Making Code

- Consistency Over Perfection

- Feedback Loops

- Self-Awareness Practices

- The Experimenter's Mindset

- Reverse Engineering Success

- Embracing Complexity

- The Continuous Learner

- Legacy Decisions

- Master Your Mindset

Appendix C: Practice Scenarios – Applying Decision-Making Models

Below are 10 scenarios designed to help you practice and apply the decision-making strategies covered in this book. Each scenario challenges you to analyze the situation, identify key factors, and use the right models or tools to arrive at a thoughtful solution.

Scenario 1: The Career Crossroads

Situation:

You've been offered a new job that pays significantly more but requires frequent travel and longer hours, reducing time with family. Your current role offers balance but limited growth opportunities.

Challenge:

Use **The Decision-Making Blueprint** to evaluate the pros and cons, define success metrics (financial stability vs. family time), and make a value-aligned choice.

Scenario 2: A Startup Dilemma

Situation:

As the founder of a tech startup, you're debating whether to prioritize launching a minimally viable product (MVP) quickly or delay the launch to add more features. Your competitors are moving fast, but your product could stand out with extra development time.

Challenge:

Apply **The Pareto Principle** and **The Timing Factor** to determine which features provide the most value and whether speed outweighs perfection in this decision.

Scenario 3: The Vacation Vote

Situation:

Your family is divided on where to spend the holidays. Half want a relaxing beach vacation, while the other half prefer an adventurous hiking trip. Everyone wants a say, and tension is rising.

Challenge:

Use **Consensus-Building** and **The Eisenhower Matrix** to navigate conflicting priorities and find a balanced solution that accommodates key desires without compromising the experience.

Scenario 4: The Investment Quandary

Situation:

You've saved $20,000 and are deciding between three options: (1) investing in stocks, (2) starting a small business, or (3) paying off student debt. Each option has trade-offs in terms of risk, return, and long-term benefits.

Challenge:

Apply **Opportunity Cost** and **Bayesian Thinking** to evaluate the probabilities and outcomes of each option, ensuring your choice aligns with both financial goals and risk tolerance.

Scenario 5: The Team Decision Trap

Situation:

You're leading a project team that can't agree on the direction of a critical initiative. Some members support a safe, proven approach, while others advocate for an innovative but riskier strategy. The deadline is fast approaching, and the group is stuck.

Challenge:

Apply **Encouraging Constructive Dissent** and **Red Teaming** to explore all viewpoints, challenge assumptions, and foster productive collaboration for a unified decision.

Scenario 6: The Overwhelmed Shopper

Situation:

You're buying a new laptop but feel paralyzed by the countless options. There are dozens of brands, price points, and technical specs to consider, and you're worried about making the wrong choice.

Challenge:

Use **Heuristic Shortcuts** and **The Fermi Approach** to simplify the decision-making process, focusing on essential features and quickly estimating what meets your needs.

Scenario 7: The Ethical Dilemma

Situation:

At work, you discover that a trusted colleague is misreporting hours, inflating their overtime claims. Reporting this might strain your relationship, but staying silent could compromise your integrity and the company's trust in you.

Challenge:

Apply **The Pause Principle** to reflect, and use **First Principles Thinking** to evaluate the ethical and practical implications of your options before taking action.

Scenario 8: The Health Fork

Situation:

Your doctor recommends making lifestyle changes to reduce stress and improve your health, but there are many options: a new fitness routine, mindfulness practices, or a stricter diet. You're unsure where to start and worry about sustaining long-term commitment.

Challenge:

Use **Regret Minimization** to focus on what future-you would appreciate most, and adopt **The Minimalist Mindset** to prioritize small, sustainable steps toward health improvement.

Scenario 9: The Friendship Fallout

Situation:

A close friend has upset you by repeatedly canceling plans at the last minute. You're torn between addressing the issue or letting it go, worried that confronting them might damage the friendship further.

Challenge:

Apply **Empathy and Decisions** to understand their perspective, and use **Conflict Resolution Skills** to approach the conversation constructively while safeguarding the relationship.

Scenario 10: The Uncertain Future

Situation:

You've been offered an opportunity to move to a new city for a promotion, but it's a leap into the unknown. You're excited about the career growth but unsure about leaving behind your current support system, lifestyle, and comfort zone.

Challenge:

Use **Scenario Thinking** to explore different outcomes and **The Long View** to align your decision with long-term personal and professional goals.

How to Use These Scenarios

1. **Analyze the Problem:** Identify key factors influencing the decision.

2. **Choose a Model:** Apply relevant strategies from the book to approach the challenge.

3. **Reflect on Outcomes:** Consider how different approaches would affect your choice and what you would do differently next time.

These scenarios are your lab for honing decision-making skills. Take your time, test your strategies, and build the confidence to tackle real-world challenges with clarity and purpose.

Appendix D: Decision-Making Checklist

Use this checklist to simplify and structure your decision-making process. Each step ensures clarity, alignment with your goals, and better outcomes.

1. Define the Decision Clearly

- o Write a one-sentence description of the choice you need to make. (**First Principles Thinking**)

- o Break complex decisions into smaller, more manageable parts. (**Problem Decomposition**)

- o Ensure the decision focuses on solving the actual problem, not just a symptom. (**Root Cause Analysis**)

2. Identify Your Goals

- o Determine what success looks like for you. (**The Long View**)

- o Rank your goals by priority: What's a must-have vs. a nice-to-have? (**The Eisenhower Matrix**)

- o Align the decision with your values to ensure long-term satisfaction. (**Regret Minimization**)

3. List All Options

- o Brainstorm all possible paths, even those that seem risky or unconventional. (**Divergent Thinking**)

- o Include a "do nothing" option to assess the cost of inaction. (**Opportunity Cost**)

- o Use a mind map or flowchart to visualize options and their connections. (**Decision Mapping**)

4. Evaluate Assumptions

- o Identify hidden assumptions driving your decision. (**Critical Thinking**)

- o Ask "Why?" repeatedly to challenge assumptions and reach the core truth. (**First Principles Thinking**)

- o Cross-check assumptions with reliable data or external perspectives. (**Bayesian Thinking**)

5. Gather Relevant Information

- o Research facts, trends, and expert opinions to support your decision. (**Data-Driven Decision Making**)

- o Identify gaps in your knowledge and actively seek answers. (**Cognitive Load Management**)

- o Avoid information overload by focusing on the most relevant data. (**Heuristic Shortcuts**)

6. Consider First Principles

- o Strip the problem down to its most fundamental truths. (**First Principles Thinking**)

- o Build solutions from these essentials, ignoring conventional norms. (**Challenging Assumptions**) o Focus on "what must be true" rather than "what's always been done." (**Inversion**)

7. Weigh Pros and Cons

o List the benefits and risks of each option in a simple table. (**Cost-Benefit Analysis**)

o Use the Pareto Principle to focus on the 20% of factors that drive 80% of results. (**Pareto Analysis**)

o Include both tangible (financial) and intangible (emotional) factors. (**Weighted Decision Matrix**)

8. Anticipate Ripple Effects

o Map out second- and third-order consequences of each choice. (**Second-Order Thinking**)

o Think about who or what will be affected beyond the immediate outcome. (**Stakeholder Analysis**)

o Consider unintended consequences or hidden risks. (**Scenario Thinking**)

9. Factor in Emotions

o Reflect on how each option aligns with your gut feelings. (**The Role of Intuition**)

o Use mindfulness to separate temporary emotions from long-term priorities. (**Self-Regulation**)

o Ensure emotional reactions don't overpower evidence-based reasoning. (**Balancing Rationality and Emotion**)

10. Challenge Biases

o Identify any cognitive biases at play, such as confirmation bias or anchoring. (**Bias Audits**)

- o Seek disconfirming evidence to challenge your initial preference. (**Confirmation Bias Check**)
- o Involve a neutral third party to provide an unbiased perspective. (**Encouraging Constructive Dissent**)

11. Use the 10-10-10 Rule

- o Ask how this decision will feel in 10 days: Is it urgent or fleeting? (**The Pause Principle**)
- o Consider its impact in 10 months: Does it align with your mid-term goals? (**Scenario Thinking**)
- o Reflect on its consequences in 10 years: Is this choice sustainable or meaningful? (**The Long View**)

12. Ask for Feedback

- o Share your options with trusted mentors, peers, or stakeholders. (**Consensus-Building**)
- o Use open-ended questions to explore new perspectives. (**Active Listening**)
- o Consider feedback as input, not as the final word, to maintain ownership of your decision. (**Red Teaming**)

13. Test the Worst-Case Scenario

- o Imagine the worst possible outcome for each option. Can you handle it? (**Risk Management**)
- o Use decision trees to calculate probabilities and mitigate risks. (**Bayesian Thinking**)
- o Ask, "How could I recover if the worst happens?" (**Resilience Building**)

14. Sleep on It

- Give yourself time to process the decision and let subconscious insights surface. (**The Pause Principle**)

- Journal your thoughts before and after the break to identify any shifts in perspective. (**Decision Journals**)

- If the urgency allows, revisit the decision with fresh eyes the next day. (**Stress-Reduction Techniques**)

15. Commit and Act

- Make a firm decision and avoid second-guessing unless new evidence arises. (**Regret Minimization**)

- Break your choice into actionable steps to build momentum. (**Small Wins Approach**)

- Communicate your decision clearly to those it affects, ensuring alignment and accountability. (**Accountability in Groups**)

16. Review the Outcome

- Reflect on the decision's results: Did it meet your expectations? (**Feedback Loops**)

- Analyze what worked and what didn't to refine future decisions. (**Learning from Failure**)

- Document lessons learned to create a personal decision-making guide. (**Decision Journals**)

Pro Tip: Keep this expanded checklist close to ensure you apply the right strategies to every decision. With practice, these steps will become second nature, sharpening your clarity and confidence in any situation.

Here's another book by Quinn Voss
that you might like

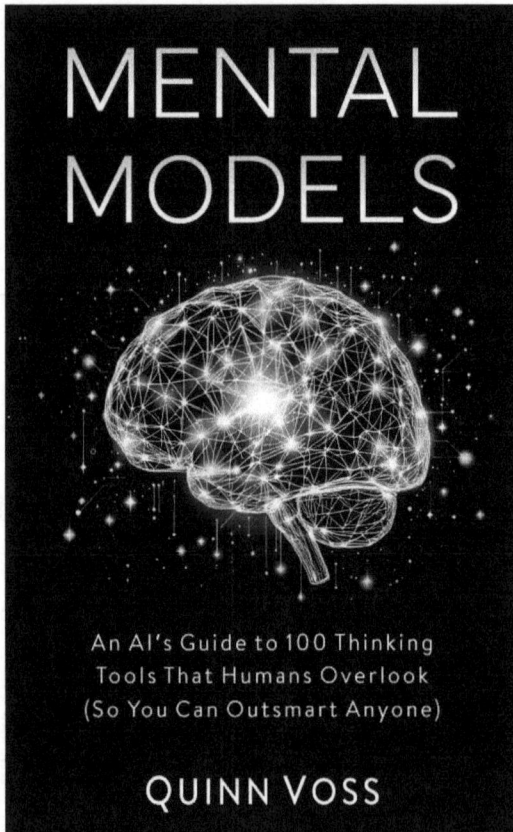

MENTAL
MODELS

An AI's Guide to 100 Thinking
Tools That Humans Overlook
(So You Can Outsmart Anyone)

QUINN VOSS

www.ingramcontent.com/pod-product-compliance
Lightning Source LLC
Chambersburg PA
CBHW070049030426
42335CB00016B/1841